1153

To love at all is to be vulnerable. Love anything, and your heart will certainly be wrung and possibly be broken. If you want to make sure of keeping it intact, you must give your heart to no one. . . . Wrap it carefully with hobbies and little luxuries; avoid all entanglements; lock it up safe in casket . . . of your own selfishness. . . . [There] it will not be broken; it will become unbreakable, impenetrable, irredeemable.

—C. S. Lewis
The Four Loves

THE
SEASONS
OF
FRIENDSHIP

A Search for Intimacy

Ruth Senter

Zondervan Publishing House
Grand Rapids, Michigan

Zondervan Publishing House, 1415 Lake Drive, S.E.,
Grand Rapids, Michigan 49506

THE SEASONS OF FRIENDSHIP
© 1982 by The Zondervan Corporation
Grand Rapids, Michigan

Library of Congress Cataloging in Publication Data

Senter, Ruth Hollinger
    The seasons of friendship.

      1. Women—Religious life. 2. Senter, Ruth Hollinger.
3. Christian biography—United States. 4. Friendship. I. Title.

BV4527.S36 1982	248.8'43	82-8565
ISBN 0-310-38830-9		AACR2

Edited by Julie Ackerman Link and Judith E. Markham
Designed by Kim Koning

Printed in the United States of America

84 85 86 87 88 — 10 9 8 7 6 5 4

To all who love gently
And risk willingly.
And especially to the One
Who taught us how.

Contents

The following story is a mosaic of people and places—real individuals, authentic locations, true drama. Sometimes in the process of recreating events, forms must be altered in order to protect. Details may be manipulated. Truth may not.

Here then is my mosaic. I have clipped, chiseled, and rearranged in order to construct it with transparency. Look at the pieces. Explore their meaning. Forget their identity. Above all, please stand back and gaze upon the whole.

Feel with me the winter past—the bitter winds that preceded change. Oneness threatened. Communion broken. Relationships born and buried before the season's shift. Buds still dormant within the branch. Growth factories held in check by arctic blasts.

But then came spring—and nothing was ever the same.

Equinox

It started out as normal banquet table talk. Fun. Light. Nothing too serious. None of us knew each other very well, but that was okay because we could hide behind the brown nutmeg candles and the arrangement of goldenrod and dried milkweed. We had just about exhausted the subjects of weather and children when someone from over the nutmeg candles fired the question. "Ruth, do you enjoy women?" I almost dropped my white ironstone coffee cup.

My brain did a sort of panic alert. *What kind of question is that? Certainly not the kind you ask the guest speaker at your women's fall kickoff. If I didn't enjoy women, why would I be here in the first place?*

"I, well—I—um—why do you ask?"

"Because there are some women who don't like each other you know." With the deliberation of a courtroom lawyer, my stranger friend across the table delivered her evidence.

"Where are friendships between women? Deep commitments? We're all committed to men. It starts in high school. My high school daughter doesn't care how many girlfriends she has. Status is how many guys ask her out. Same way in college. Saturday night with the girls was an old-maid's party. Dinner with a man was first-class entertainment. Ever heard a woman say, "I'd much rather talk with men than women? Men are much more interesting.' I hear it all the time. Where's our loyalty to one another? We're too busy competing, that's where it is."

She's obviously chosen her theme. Probably has played it before, I thought. Fortunately for me, the parade of winter fashions interrupted our conversation. I didn't have time to answer, and I had no idea what I would have said anyhow. It wasn't the kind of question one is asked every day. By the time the last burgundy suede sandal had disappeared down the ramp and the raspberry sherbet had vanished from our plates, no one remembered the question. I breathed easier and focused my attention on the three points of my after-dinner talk.

Women don't enjoy each other. Another over-generalization, I thought to myself as I drove home later that night. *It's not that women don't enjoy each other. It's just that God has magnetized us toward men. After all, he didn't put two women in the garden of Eden. Must have been a women's libber across the table. Probably had some big disappointment with men so now her theme is sisterhood.*

I flipped my thoughts to Milt Rosenberg, my favorite nighttime radio talk-show host. "The oil crisis: true or false?" Now there was an issue worth worrying about. I was captivated by the debate. These men knew what they were talking about. They'd served their time. They'd done their homework. They had impressive credentials: head of the Petroleum Industry Research Foundation, member of the Federal Energy Administration, professor of economics at Massachusetts Institute of Technology, dean of petroleum consultants and adviser to governments.

"How'd your evening go?" Mark was waiting up for me in his favorite wing chair. For the next thirty minutes we discussed OPEC, the government's phased decontrol program, and nuclear energy as an alternative to oil. That's one of the things I like about Mark. He always enjoys issues. He was impressed with my knowledge on the subject—at least he told me he was. It didn't matter that I'd learned it all during my ninety minute ride home from the banquet.

"Oh yes," I added as I was about to drift off to sleep. "Had a nice evening with the ladies, too. The candles smelled like nutmeg. Someone asked me if I enjoyed women. Strange question isn't it? Don't think I'll lose any sleep over that one."

Actually I couldn't afford to lose sleep over much of anything right then. Another week and it was retreat time. "A semi-guest speaker," I called myself. Tucked away in a corner of the program was a mini-session with my name beside it.

"Learn lots," Mark said as he kissed me good-bye in front of the TWA terminal. "I'll try." Little did I realize the significance of our exchange as I picked up my suitcase and headed for gate H7.

I was already feeling a little insecure by the time the cabby deposited me in front of my hotel. The stop under the hotel portico was the first time he'd applied his brakes during the entire ride from the airport. Evidently he was into challenges. Our zigzag through the restrained lines of rush-hour traffic convinced me that he was definitely Grand Prix material.

"Nerves. Calm down." I tried to talk myself into composure as I ran a brush through my hair, grabbed my jacket, and rushed downstairs to the staff dinner. However, my insides were still doing zigzags through the rush-hour traffic as I sat down in the first empty seat I could spot.

"Hello. I'm Ruth Senter." I greeted my neighbor to my left and looked squarely into a face I'd seen smiling from book jackets and magazine pages for years. She didn't need to tell me her name, but she did anyhow. Suddenly I could not think of another thing to say. She held out a perfectly manicured hand to welcome me. Her nail polish matched the mauve color of her blouse. I immediately remembered that I'd forgotten to do my nails. They looked rough and anemic. I was grateful that the white linen tablecloth was long enough to hide my hands.

I had a hard time pulling my mind away from silk, mauve-colored blouses and perfectly manicured nails. By the time I did, the discussion had moved to Hawaii. She'd just returned from a month-long speaking vacation circuit on the islands with her husband.

When she asked what I'd done with my summer, I told her that we had camped with our children at White Pines State Park, about two hours east of where we live. "Our children are really into tents and campfires. Does a lot for family togetherness to sleep in a tent when the rain is sliding down the hillside right into your warm, dry, down-filled sleeping bags. Lessons we'd never want our kids to miss." I felt I had to apologize. I wanted to hide our campfire and tent under the white linen tablecloth along with my anemic-looking nails. How unglamorous it all must seem.

Someone asked about her books. She had just sent manuscript number seven to the publisher—had finished it under a palm tree in Hawaii. *Who couldn't write a book under a palm tree in Hawaii.*

I remembered my only book manuscript, typed to the tune of "M-i-c-k-e-y M-o-u-s-e" blaring from a three-year-old's room across the hall. Visions of book writing preschool style flashed in front of my chicken kiev. Toy soldiers marched through my carefully typed, ready-for-the-editor pages. "Matchbox" fire engines screamed under my desk and across my *Writer's Manual of Style,* looking for the fire. Suddenly I felt very noble.

What about her children? I wanted to ask the question, but I didn't. I knew there were five. How did they fit in with seven books, whirlwind tours of the islands, and speaking circuits that crisscrossed the world? Who fixed the peanut butter sandwiches and served on the PTA committees? Who went to district band competition and the first home game of the season? Somebody had to be suffering—missing out on something. It didn't appear to be mother. I mentally complimented myself on my dedication.

The after-dinner speech of welcome was as smooth and polished as my famous neighbor's mauve fingernails. The retreat organizer introduced her guests. Their credentials were impressive. I almost dreaded to have my name called.

What am I doing here? This is out of my class. Another league. At that moment the knowledge that God had planted me there was clouded by what I considered my inadequacies. I left the luncheon feeling about three feet high. The seven-book author graciously invited me to call if I ever visited her hometown.

Credentials were not the only thing I struggled with that night. There was also the unresolved matter of roommates. I had hoped for some privacy—concentration time for my seminar. No one knew, I was sure, how much emotional energy it costs to be a public speaker. For those who didn't have to be a fountainhead of ideas and information by 10:00 A.M., bedtime lost all significance.

"We've got a full house," the hostess greeted me as I registered at the front desk. "We knew you wouldn't mind sharing." As I rode the elevator to the fourth floor, I wondered who my roommate would be.

I didn't have to wonder long. The key clicked in the lock as I was taking off my coat, and suddenly I was involved. There wasn't a moment's hesitation on her part. "Hi. I'm Ellen. Gee, I'm glad you're here. It's going to be nice to have someone to talk to."

Ellen was like a newspaper just waiting to be unfolded and read. By the end of our late night coffee and pie in the hotel coffee shop, I'd heard her entire life in review. It was entitled "victim."

For as long as she could remember, Ellen had been a victim—of a childhood without love, of an unhappy marriage that had ended three years earlier, of two undisciplined children, of an unjust legal system, of food she couldn't resist (and an over-sized body to show for it), of a grocery store that trapped her into a three-by-five cashier's cubicle for eight hours a day. Even her commitment to Christ, like the other parts of her world, seemed caught in her clogged machinery of life. She just couldn't seem to make it work.

Fortunately for Ellen, I'd just completed a personal study on what the Bible has to say about discipline and self-control. "The fruit of the spirit is self control—For God hasn't given us the spirit of timidity, but of power and love and discipline—If any one considers himself religious and yet does not keep a tight rein on his tongue (you eat and talk with your tongue), he deceives himself and his religion is worthless." The kernels of truth kept popping out of my head and falling exactly where Ellen needed them.

Any hopes for refueling my body with a sufficient amount of sleep had long since vanished. Here was a person who needed help. Ellen listened attentively as she served herself another piece of apple pie and watched me diagram ten steps to self-control on the back of her napkin. I thought up the ten steps as I went along, but the finished product looked impressive. Ellen seemed eager to put

my suggestions to work and tucked into her program book my
secret code for untangling the knotted threads of her life. We had
another cup of coffee, with cream and sugar, and then caught the
elevator for the fourth floor.

As we were getting ready for bed, I thought of some books she
should read on the subject. Ellen got out her inspired napkin and I
added the titles. If Ellen didn't pull herself out of the quagmire, it
certainly wouldn't be my fault. I prayed with her, thanking God for
His support in her improvement projects. We turned out our light
and I tried for some sleep—about three hours later than my calculated expectations.

By the time the weekend retreat was over I felt that Ellen had
permanently lodged herself under my skin, drawing out my vital
supply of energy. The problem was that Ellen kept returning to
ground we had already plowed. And most of this plowing took
place in the coffee shop. I finally suggested to her that we sit somewhere else to talk. My funds were running low, and besides, I
didn't need the coffee. Ellen volunteered to buy me a cup of tea. I
gave in and she ended up with a pecan roll as well.

It was becoming more and more evident to me that perhaps
what Ellen needed was someone else to take charge of her life for
her. She didn't seem to have the commitment to do it for herself.
"Ellen, I'm not passing this bread basket to you. You don't need a
second roll," I said half-teasingly at the closing banquet. Ellen
laughed and took the roll anyhow.

I reviewed the situation to Mark later at home as I smugly
unpacked my size nine dresses. "Women don't want to take charge
of their own lives," I lamented. "Do you know how many overweight women there are? And yet all we do is go out for coffee.
What we need at women's retreats are some seminars on self-
control, personal management, world hunger, involvement in in-
ternational affairs—topics that make us think, consider the issues,
get ourselves organized. You ever been to a men's retreat where you
had demonstrations in auto-mechanics, house painting, or a seminar on how to trim your moustache?"

Mark was amused.

"I guess I should read some books about sisterhood or

friendship or something." I was beginning to feel a little guilty for my lofty pronouncements upon those of my own sex. Detached formalities had always been about as deep as my commitment to sisterhood went.

"Maybe you should write one." Mark dropped the idea as casually as if he were suggesting pizza for dinner.

I looked to see if he was serious. I could tell he was. The seed was in the ground. It would germinate later—months later—in the throes of transition. Uprootedness. No strings attached anywhere any more. . . .

I heard the phone ringing from somewhere behind the barricade of brown boxes marked "Kitchen. This side up." *Somebody knows we're in.* First sign of life. It was almost like hearing my baby's heartbeat for the first time. I desperately needed to hear that ring. I scrambled through the corrugated obstacle course and reached eagerly for the gold trimline that had just been installed hours earlier.

The voice on the other end sounded cordial enough. "I know you just moved in, but we thought you might be interested anyway. Wednesday is lunch out with the girls. A group of us from church goes together. We'd love to have you join us. Here's my number if you can squeeze it into your day tomorrow."

I thanked her, scribbled down her number, and stuffed it into my miscellaneous file which, like most everything else in the house, had yet to find a permanent resting place. I never called her back.

"I don't understand why you didn't take an hour or two off today and go out for lunch." Mark introduced the topic from the top rung of the ladder where he was hanging drapery rods. "It would have been a good chance to get acquainted."

I muttered something about "bad timing—too much to do—have to get things settled first." But something inside me said, *Boxes will wait. Some reasons go deeper than unpacked moving crates.* It was as though Linda's call had reactivated the yellow caution light in my brain. It flashed out its warning: Enter at your own risk. Potential hurt. Proceed with care. Serve people but don't give them your soul. Use your head when it comes to relationships. Protect your heart.

Part of me wanted to ignore the light, rush right out into the traffic, scoop up all the friends I could find, hold tightly to them, and say, "I love you. I need you. Let's be friends." The other part of me was bolted to the curb where things were safe and certain. People don't usually get hurt if they stay on the safety island. But then they don't get across the street either.

Where did my flashing caution light come from—the one that kept me from risking? I knew the time had come to begin my answer.

The quest led me back—way back—to roads of my past. Sometimes the journey back was not easy. It resurrected feelings and faces. Some painful. Some pure delight. Some so far away and so long forgotten that they were but particles on a distant horizon. Some were reminders of winters past. But when God's timing turned winter to spring, the past and the present merged, and suddenly I realized that the book had been written. Now it was simply time to put it down on paper.

PART I

Winter
Past

·⚙ 1 ⚙·

Empty
Holes

I heard the gentle swish of water—a rhythmic cadence lapping itself on the beach just beyond the trailer walls. My sluggish brain struggled to put the noise into context. Where? When? Why? How? Gradually the scene came into focus.

Midsummer. Morning. A quiet Christian retreat center in northwest Indiana. A family in transit—pulling up deep root systems from the red clay of southern Alabama to transplant them to the Kansas wheat fields. An available spot beneath the pines for our tiny eighteen-foot trailer. A few days rest from the road. Swimming. Fishing. Sun and shade.

I scrambled over my two sleeping brothers, pulled on some clothes, and headed out to investigate my new world. The sky was almost as blue as the Alabama skies I'd looked into all my life. The pines were not as tall and straight, but pines nevertheless. We had lakes in Alabama, too, but I was much more at home with creeks that crawled through the woods, fell over dead logs and clumpy undergrowth, and, during the rainy season, cut the roads in two. You could always tell the time of the year, the conditions of the crops, and the mood of the weather by the character of the creek.

But I'd said good-bye to that creek. And here in front of me was a lake—calm and subdued in the predawn. I didn't want to disturb it—at least not yet.

Right now in this peaceful little spot where the beach turned into the forest it was just me and the birds. I liked it that way. I watched the tiny, winged creatures as they fluttered through the pines. They were strange birds, with names I didn't know and color combinations I'd never seen. Back home in Alabama I knew most of the birds, the result of long Saturday afternoons our family had spent walking in the woods. I looked for familiar feathers and found none.

The slight stirring in the pines startled me out of my bird reveries. The first thing I noticed about the girl who stepped out onto the beach was that she was not my age—probably six or seven years older. Maybe she had a younger sister somewhere for me to pal around with.

The second thing I noticed about her were her eyes. They reminded me of a reflecting pool I had seen once at the home of a wealthy family in the faraway town of Brewton. Deep. Clear. With a rich lining of blue behind them. I thought she was very beautiful.

"Mind if I sit here with you? I come here every morning to read my Bible. Now you've found my secret spot. But that's okay. We can share it. It's the most beautiful little nook anywhere around the lake, and I know 'cause yesterday I walked all the way around it. Are you here camping with your family?" Her voice sounded like wind chimes.

I immediately forgot about southern pines and rambling creeks. Here was someone who made me interested in right now. I wanted to know what she found on the other side of the lake, what the symbol printed on her sweat shirt stood for, and where she had gotten a bright red Bible. But those questions would wait.

Joan sat down beside me on a little patch of elevated rock just beyond where the sunny beach and the shadowy woods met. She didn't seem to mind sharing her rock, and I felt no inclination to move on. She picked up a stick and began to create dust doodles. "Can you guess what this is? Tell me about yourself. Where'd you come from? By the way, I like your braids. They match the brown in your eyes.

"Me? I'm from Michigan. Our high school youth group from church comes here camping every summer. Did you see that fish jump? This lake has some of the best stock of lake trout. We had some for dinner the other night—cooked over an open fire. Do you like to fish? Maybe you and I could take a boat out this afternoon and test our skills. Why don't we go ask your mom?" Her blue eyes sparkled at me.

From that moment on we were friends. Where Joan went, I followed close behind. And she seemed to like having me there. She bought me ice cream at the canteen, gave me a sweat shirt like hers with her youth group emblem on it, signed my autograph book "To Ruth Ann, my special little friend," looked at the school pictures of all twenty-four people who had just finished fourth grade with me. She explained Psalm 23 to me from her youth director's point of view, put night crawlers on the hook at the end of my fishing pole, and taught me to make a dandelion chain from the handfuls of bright yellow flowers we gathered one afternoon on our walk around the lake. One day she even let me wear her gold junior class ring with the ruby stone in the middle. It fit perfectly on my thumb.

At night, in my dinner-table-turned-bed, I would close my eyes and return to Alabama—to our little white house squatting in the middle of that magnificent stand of pines that stretched for acres over the red clay soil—and dream of my warm, friendly schoolhouse with its knotty pine walls and an artesian well out back that could refresh the day no matter how dry and parched the air happened to be.

In the morning I would wake up in Indiana to the lapping of waves, and I'd remember Joan. Her friendship pulled me from my past and sat me down squarely in the present. I'd gulp down my Cheerios and rush out to find Joan. I knew she'd be waiting for me down by the rock where early in the morning the sun and shadows met.

As quickly and silently as she walked into my life, she was gone, snatched away into oblivion. It had only been three short days, but in that time I had wrapped up my heart and given it to Joan.

Now I kicked the ashes of a blazing campfire grown cold—the

circle of warmth where last night I'd sat with Joan and her friends. We'd sung half the night away. The campfire had drawn us all in from the chilly night, and the happiness of that moment had held us there until long after my bedtime. Mother had given me special permission to stay up. In fact, she and daddy had even walked down and joined us. Joan had gone out of her way to invite them. I thought she'd done it especially for me. Looking across the fire at my family, my happiness had been complete.

Today that circle of warmth lost all significance. The logs were just a figuration of cold, dead wood. The fire, an ash heap. The ground was full of tent stake holes and the grassy areas were matted and mashed into the dirt. Joan was gone. I found the holes where her tent had been and felt like I was looking at the holes in my heart.

"I know you miss Joan." Mother's arms pulled me close as I tried to choke down my Cheerios. I cried on her soft shoulders. Outside, the trailer was hitched up and ready to go. I had to go back, just one more time. Final farewells. I ran down to our rock. In my mind I saw Joan sitting there with her sparkling eyes and her soft voice that sounded like wind chimes. But today, the rock was just a patch of lifeless gray slate. This morning the sun and shadows didn't even meet. It was all shadow.

I climbed into our brown and white Dodge and headed west with my family, but part of my heart stayed there beside a calm, little lake in northwestern Indiana. It was days before that part of my heart caught up with the rest of me. Meanwhile, I wondered how something that had brought so much happiness could possibly hurt so much when it was gone. The pain never completely went away.

But time teaches you what to do with pain. You avoid it. Close your eyes to it. Don't look when the needle comes toward your arm. Keep your fingers out of the fire. Insulate. Isolate. Insure. Layer upon layer build your protection against pain. So next time there won't be any strings that pull your heart apart, no tent stake holes that close in around a circle of warmth now grown cold.

And the seasons ride out their orb, rotating with the earth. Summer is lost. You blot out the past because the memories hurt. A friend is gone. You close your eyes to emotional entanglements of the present and protect yourself against future loss. Compensate for relationships. Replace. Produce. Perform. Possess. But do not love deeply. Loving deeply may hurt.

Gradually, in place of the celebration of intimacy that began in a garden called Eden, you erect an island. A lonely place of solitude. Private. Peaceful. Without involvement. But also devoid of love, laughter, and freedom that throws caution to the wind and allows hearts to be divinely bound to one another.

And so you sit out the winters of your life, unencumbered by relationships, removed from the pain, safe from the loss. The intimacy for which God created you is boarded up and stashed away on a remote island until, in another season, you learn to risk again.

When the Colors Change

"That will be three dollars and ninety-five cents," the lady with the blue eyes and the short blond hair said to me from the other side of the counter. I unwrapped the five-dollar bill I had curled up in my sweaty palm, handed it over the glass jar of colored bubble gum, and waited for my change.

"You must be the new preacher's daughter. You look like your daddy. He stopped by here last night for gas. We're glad to have you in our community. You bought the Bell's place, didn't you? Your dad says he has plans for the church to be built right next to your house. You're a long way from Kansas. But then, you've lived in Alabama before haven't you? It's a great state." I nodded and she continued.

"Now let's see. You look to be about the same age as my niece, Virginia. Ninth grade? Well, what do you know? Same age and her daddy's a preacher, too. Virginia's a fine girl, if I do say so myself. Smart. Plays the piano. Youngest homecoming queen Reston High ever had. You'll like her. Everybody does. Good Christian girl, too. I think you two had better get together." She smiled at me from over the colorful bubble-gum balls.

27

I could tell this conversation could go on indefinitely. Apparently the storekeeper-postmistress had all the time in the world for morning chitchat. But I didn't. I politely excused myself, stuffed the newly purchased box of soap into the basket of my bike, and headed around the curve and down the road toward home.

By my first day of school at Reston High, Virginia Wilcox was already something of a legend in my mind. After her aunt's impressive accounts, I'd gone home and looked her up in the yearbook that a neighbor down the road had lent to me. Her credentials looked impeccable. So did her face—a perfect oval framed by long, coal-black hair, set off by deep, dark eyes and a wide, white smile. Something about the sweetness of her smile made me feel that Virginia was a friend who could be trusted. That trust would have no small consequence in the days and years to come. . . .

The night of the first football game of the season I felt an unsettledness—almost like the stars might forget to come out or the moon wouldn't get hung up in its proper place. There was no routine yet. No secure little spot where I knew I'd feel safe. No order to the evening. No last week to look back to and say, "See, it went all right last time. Don't worry about tonight." There were no guarantees that somewhere in the crowd there'd be someone who was looking for me, someone who would call out to me, "Hey, Ruth Ann. Come sit with us."

I wanted desperately to belong—to be as natural to the scene as the goalposts were to the football field, as comfortable and easy as the fall winds that blew down over the night; as special as the cheerleaders, as much at home as the giant bulldog mascot that guarded the scoreboard at the south end of the field. I needed to be a part.

Daddy's car pulled away. I looked at the crowd before me. Intimidating. Unknown. A collage of strange faces. I'd met a few people during those first days of school, but somehow that fact provided very little comfort as I hesitated at the foot of the terraced rows of spectators. "The only way to make friends is to go where they are," my mother had said as I nervously arranged my semi-straight brown hair over my blue jacket collar and ran for the car where daddy was waiting. "You'll be okay," she called out to me. I wished I could believe her. Things were just too tentative yet. Too unsure to trust. I would have to muddle through somehow.

And muddle through I did. Straight ahead as though I knew exactly where I was going. I panicked at the thought that I could walk the entire length of those bleachers and not find one person I knew. "But somewhere along the line you have to get out of the boat and start to swim," was another of my parents' bits of wisdom. I remembered the line and wondered if this time I was going to drown. I clutched my brown suede purse for support.

Suddenly I caught a signal. A wave about halfway up the stands. "Hey, Ruth Ann. Come on up and sit with us." Suddenly everything was okay. It was as though someone had wrapped a warm blanket around me on a cold, winter night.

"Move over everybody." It was Virginia who sang out the order. I squeezed in beside her. "Gee, I'm glad you came. Have some popcorn." She dumped half her bag into my hands. "Isn't this exciting? We're supposed to have one of the best teams in the county this year. See number thirteen? He's my brother. Where was it your accent came from? That's okay, we'll teach you to speak southern. Just give us a couple weeks. Ya'll come. . . ." She prolonged her "Ya'l-l-l" just for the effect. Everyone laughed. I wasn't sure if they were laughing at her or at me, but right then it didn't even matter. I'd found security, at least for the moment.

Virginia watched over me that night like mother-protector. She matched names with faces for me. Gave me a rundown on all the football players and varsity cheerleaders. Briefed me on the hard teachers and "the softies." Directed me through the crowds to the concession stand and the washrooms, and always said, "Move over, you guys. Make room for Ruth Ann," when we came back to our seats.

"She makes you feel that she really cares about you," I said to my mother later that night as I rehearsed to her every important and unimportant detail of the evening. "I like her. Everyone likes her. No wonder. Lucky for me that we know her aunt. I think that helped."

In the days that followed I decided that whether Virginia's aunt knew you or not didn't really matter to Virginia. She liked everybody—made you feel that you were the only person in the world. She looked at you when you talked. Laughed at your jokes. Asked questions like, "Now what was it your dad was doing in Kansas?" or "How does your brother like tenth grade?" She made me feel that the blue plaid hand-me-down skirt I wore really was neat looking and that having a Kansas non-accent was really something special after all.

"Are you glad your dad's a preacher?" she asked me one day at break as we sipped our Cokes and munched corn curls. We always got Coke and corn curls at break. It was funny how we kept finding that we liked the same things. "I'm kinda happy about dad being a preacher. Makes me feel that he's really helping people. And that's an important thing in life, don't you think?"

I was always amazed that Virginia thought so much. She had opinions about everything and anything. "Smart girl," I told mother one day. "Almost like she belongs in tenth grade. She got the only A in English yesterday. How can she know so much?"

Mother didn't answer my question, but I could tell that she was glad Virginia and I were getting to be such good friends. "I think they're good for each other. Two of a kind. I'm happy she's found a Christian friend," I heard her tell daddy one night. I knew she was talking about Virginia and me.

I watched Virginia extra closely one afternoon in school as she rapped on the teachers' big, brown desk and called the 4-H Club meeting to order. Virginia was the president, and Mrs. Dean, our sponsor, said she'd never seen such a well-run and enthusiastic chapter. Everyone knew it was because of Virginia. She was totally loyal and patriotic to whatever she did.

"Betty Lou Blackwell . . . Doris Gilmore . . . Susie White. . . ." I felt a sudden pride as I watched Virginia call roll and make the appropriate marks in the brown attendance book. She was *my* friend. Give us half a chance and we always found each other, even if we happened to be at opposite ends of the hall when the bell rang. She looked so strong and sure of herself in front of all the seventh, eighth, and ninth grade girls—like she knew exactly what to do with her hands; and that even if she did the wrong things with them, it would still be all right because she was Virginia—likeable, loveable, capable Virginia.

When she came to my name she drawled out "Hollinger." She looked up at me and winked. It was our own private little joke. We were always arguing about the proper way to pronounce my last name—the southern way with a hard "g" or the Kansas way with a soft "g." This time she won, and we both knew it. There was no way I could correct her like I usually did. Hard "g" or soft "g," it didn't even matter. What mattered was that there was something between us that no one else shared. It was almost as though Virginia was reserved for me. No one else understood.

Overall, I was convinced that Virginia was a genuine Christian. One noon we spent lunch hour discussing whether we would know each other when we got to heaven. Virginia seemed well assured that heaven would be her final destination. Meanwhile, she seemed to live consistently. I thought her dad must be proud of her—an example for his church to see. I had no doubts in my mind about Virginia.

"How about an overnight at my house this weekend?" Virginia bounced up to me one morning as I got off the bus. "It's okay with my mom. She'll write your mom a note. The barbecue is this Friday night. It's a big production. Everybody comes from everywhere. Makes lots of money for the school. It's really fun. Lots of music, games, stuff to buy. You could come home with me on the bus and then my folks would bring us back for the barbecue. Oh, yes, there are lots of cute boys, too. Some come over from Evergreen High School. That's about thirty miles up the road toward Montgomery."

If there were boys, I was definitely interested. Virginia and I had each made our pick one afternoon as we watched the football team work out. Both boys we chose were eleventh graders, but that didn't matter. We decided Bruce and Robert were the cutest boys in the whole school and definitely worth watching.

Our infatuation didn't amount to much more than monitoring their every move, scratching their names and numbers on our notebooks, and wishing we were tenth graders so that our heroes would at least acknowledge our existence. I always thought that was all the further our ninth-grade crushes went.

"I have a surprise for you after the barbecue tonight." Virginia's dark eyes sparkled with intrigue. "But I can't tell you till then." A late-night show on TV? A giant ice cream sundae? The scrapbook of her summer with an aunt in Atlanta that she had promised to show me sometime? I couldn't imagine, but whatever Virginia had planned, I knew it would be fun.

"You'll have a good time with Virginia," my mom had said earlier that morning as she helped me squeeze shut my blue overnight bag that I'd stuffed with enough extraneous junk to see me through two weeks of vacation. "She seems like such a nice girl. I've heard good things about her parents, too. It was kind of them to invite you, wasn't it? I love you. Have fun," she called, and I disappeared out the front door and down the porch steps toward the bus.

The night was fun. The barbecued meat was some of the best I'd ever tasted. "Special secret recipe," one of the dish-up men said. "The recipe they use in the governor's mansion up in Montgomery. Must be a spy in their kitchen." He laughed as he handed me a mountain of steaming barbecue on a red-checked paper plate. Virginia and I wasted no time devouring that steaming mountain of meat.

When the band's medley of songs of the south turned into "Dixie," Virginia and I jumped up, waved our confederate flags, and cheered so loudly my throat felt raw for the rest of the night. There was a square-dance troop in yellows and blues, a magician who kept tripping over his electrical chords, and of course, a short speech from the principal thanking the community for supporting the school.

Virginia and I wandered through the crowds, paid our quarters to knock over the duck decoys with a B-B gun or to ring the neck of the stuffed turkey, and ate more barbecue. We stood around in groups and talked to our friends or climbed to the top bleachers and scouted out the territory for numbers twelve and thirty-nine who were there somewhere, only tonight they were without their helmets and numbers.

The crowd began to thin down. The huge pans of barbecue sat empty. While we were still on the top bleacher, Virginia's mother called to us that it was time to go. I was content. It had been a fun night. I felt almost euphoric as we drove through the dark, quiet canopy of pines toward Virginia's house, secure in our friendship and confident about belonging.

"Ruth Ann and I are going to bed," Virginia said abruptly as soon as we entered the house. Suddenly she seemed almost mechanical. Calculated. Nervous. *Must be how she gets when she's tired.* I began to realize that I might be seeing a side of Virginia that had never shown up at school. "No, thank you. We're too full," she snapped back when her mother asked if we wanted a bedtime snack. "See you in the morning." And with that she closed us into her bedroom.

"Here's the deal," she whispered as she kicked off her shoes and sat down on her pink ruffled bedspread. Suddenly I felt a knot tying up my stomach. This was a Virginia I did not know. "We lay low for forty-five minutes or so and then, see this window? It opens nice and quietly. Three minutes down the road and we're at Morris's store. Here's the surprise." She stopped for effect. "Bruce and Robert are going to be there to pick us up at ten o'clock. That gives us just thirty minutes to get to sleep. Mother and daddy never check once I've closed my door. We operate on trust around here."

"But—but—" I took a deep breath. "I'm not allowed to date."

"That's okay. Neither am I. We don't call this dating. Just a tour of Watkins Park in the moonlight, and with the two cutest boys in the whole school!" She whirled around the room.

"Don't worry." Virginia was beginning to notice my lack of exuberance. "I've done it before. In fact, Bruce and I have a little routine going. I haven't told you because I wanted to surprise you and fix you up, too. Robert really does think you're cute. Bruce said so. Only he can't show it at school. It would hurt his image to notice a ninth grader.

"Now, what do you say? Shall we turn out the light and go to bed? I'm so-o-o tired." She stretched and opened her mouth in a fake yawn, trying to pretend things were normal.

Suddenly I was cold all over, even though the room was warm. "When you—when you sneak out with Bruce, where do you go?" I felt like I should be whispering under the covers. It was a dirty, dark kind of feeling.

"Oh, just riding around. Sometimes we park by the lake and watch the submarines for a while, if you know what I mean." She laughed a nervous little laugh and waited for me to join her gaiety.

"You go on, Virginia," I said in a monotone voice that came from somewhere outside me. "I don't feel very well. Think I ate too much barbecue. I'll just go to bed. Have fun." I opened my overnight bag and started to undress.

"Virginia seems like such a nice girl," mother had said this morning as she helped me zip up this very overnight bag. That seemed like a month ago, and mother seemed miles away. I wanted to run to her. To feel her warmth. To sob on her soft, trustworthy shoulders. To have her put her arms around me and tell me this was just a made-up story with a bad ending. Things like this don't happen in real life. Friends can be trusted. It's okay to think they're special. They won't disappoint you. They'll be strong for you. They'll automatically know how much it will hurt you if they let you down. I wanted so much to believe that.

"Okay, if you don't want to go." Virginia was quietly putting on her shoes again. Her clock said 9:55. She didn't even look at me. "I did it for you. Thought you'd jump at the chance. One of the cutest guys in the school, too." She threw a sweater over her shoulders, pushed open the silent window, and disappeared out into the night.

With her disappeared something else—my trust—my friendship with Virginia would never again be the same. It couldn't be. Ever.

And as the earth tracks through space and the years replace one another, you remember disappointment. Your adult mind reminds you what happens when you trust someone. They build you up to let you down, take your hopes and give them back to you in an empty paper bag. Friends seem to be what they are not and are not what they seem to be. You give of yourself to them with no second thoughts. Pure trust. No cross-examination. No scrutiny. You take them for what they seem. You believe in their authenticity. But only until reality catches up with you and shows you a different picture. Then a friend lets you down. You blame yourself for your naïveté, your friend for inconsistency. You reject act and actor, deed and doer. And you remember that you were let down once before.

And in your current disappointment you determine it will never happen again. Next time no one is going to mislead you. You will not give them the chance. You become a skeptic; you rechart your course to compensate for your diminished faith in people. Once you gave without reservation. Now you reserve the right to add up the risk, cross-examine the motives, check out the loopholes, weigh the returns. Once you expected the best; now you imagine the worst. Once you gave the benefit of the doubt; now you simply doubt.

In your skepticism you become intolerant and unforgiving. Someone's irrational season has hurt you once. You steel yourself against becoming a victim of future error. No expectations, no disappointments. See through everyone. That way you'll never be taken in. Carry a microscope. Truth is always colored. Watch for the colors, even if they're not there.

And in your skepticism you squeeze out intimacy. Intimacy embraces both virtues and inconsistencies, and inconsistencies sometimes hurt. You cannot run the risk. And so you sit out the winter of your skepticism like a field stripped of the harvest. Barren. Cold. Empty. True friendship exists only between the leather bindings of a book. The rest is just play-acting. Trust is a theory. Life is fickleness and fluctuation. Colors change. Count on no one. Save your heart.

Until in another place, at another time, when the North Pole tilts in another direction, you learn once again to trust.

3

Game Boards

For a moment I felt like the world was slipping out of control. Blurs of blues, browns, brilliant oranges, and gold moved at high speed through my peripheral vision. Greens rushed up to meet me. With my legs suspended in midair, strong, muscular flanks propelled me through the air, gobbling up space underfoot.

"Hang on. Let 'im run," a voice somewhere at the edge of the woods yelled. "Lean into him. Go with the flow." I tried desperately to remember all the amateur advice my dad had given me about horseback riding. But that was when horses were slower and we rode bareback on Sally, the gentle old mare back in Alabama that plodded along down the pasture path to round up the cows for milking time. Sally didn't even know the word gallop. That was before my encounters with professional riding stables, English saddles, and spirited quarter horses with their insatiable appetite for speed and sudden starts and stops.

Right now the name of the game was survival—a frantic struggle for balance and control. I reached for the saddle horn that wasn't there and came up with a fistful of coarse, brown hair instead. I remembered I was riding English.

I could almost feel the pulse of the stretched-out body beneath me. His neck was arched and his strong head seemed to be pulling us both through endless uncertainty. I pressed my legs into his sides and pulled hard on the reins. That much I finally did remember.

Brighton got the message. His massive frame slowed to a trot, then a walk. I could feel his sweat against my legs. I wasn't sure who had been working hardest, the horse or me.

"Hey, I'm going to sign you up for the rodeo. You might even make the big time. Not bad for an amateur." Anne laughed. Her dark, shoulder-length hair bounced as she pulled her horse to a stop beside mine, directing him with a movement so slight it was barely noticeable. Anne was a born horsewoman. She handled her horse with ease and confidence—every inch a pro.

I had little doubt about her abilities as a trail guide either. She appeared to know the territory—a comforting thought as I looked at the endless miles of forest that covered the hills.

"I've been through every nook and cranny of these parts. I started coming here when I was just a kid," she said as we headed north toward the hazy ridges that slept stretched out in the early-morning mist. They looked like nothing could disturb them. Anne named the peaks and valleys as they came into view. She was at home with the hills. This morning their majesty and gentleness drew us together.

"Come on. Let's go." She leaned forward and lifted her reins. "We've got a lot of ground to cover." This time she took the lead and Brighton followed. Slow and easy—much more my speed. Between the leafy forest walls and the branches that rubbed against my face, down moss-tufted banks, and across trickles of fresh mountain water. Actually, I was amazed that these foothills had so many mountain streams—pure, cold, and crystal clear.

"This is the runoff from the Appalachian range, the real mountains farther north," Anne observed. "The Appalachian trail cuts just east of here. You may not be aware of it yet—you have to live here for a while—but you are looking at some of the finest territory in all of eastern Pennsylvania. No wonder William Penn went to so much trouble for this land."

We came to a little clearing in the woods—a grassy slope variegated with spruce, hemlock, and pine—like someone had planned a haven of evergreen in the middle of a dense, deciduous forest.

"Let's stop. This looks like a good spot for a rest," Anne said as she tied Queens to the trunk of a pine and unsnapped the saddlebag that was stuffed with goodies to refresh hungry travelers along the trail. I felt authentic. Primitive. Pioneer. Back to nature. And terribly peaceful. Mother's Moravian sugar cake had never tasted so good. Anne handed me a steaming thermos cup of hot chocolate. I leaned back to savor the moment. I could hear a stream somewhere beyond.

I watched idly as Anne finished her hot chocolate, stretched, and then got up to care for the horses. "Sometimes this trail is hard on their feet because of all the stones." Anne pulled a hoof prick out of the saddlebag. With the gentleness of a nurse, she lifted their hooves and inspected for stones. She spoke softly to her animals, rubbed their sweaty flanks with a rubber currycomb, then topped off the ceremonies with a carrot for each.

There was both a softness and a hardness to Anne that I liked. Determined. Direct. She always appeared to know where she needed to go, but she didn't push too hard to get there—even with the animals; it was a kind of decisive gentleness.

Unlikely friends, I thought to myself as I watched Anne care for her animals and move between the horses. She was wearing black riding boots and a derby hat, tight breeches, and a green Pendleton blazer. I brushed the dust off my faded blue jeans, unaware of the contrast except to note that things like clothes didn't seem to matter to Anne. They were a normal part of her life and she didn't apologize or draw attention to them.

I couldn't remember a beginning with Anne. As a country girl from Alabama, recently transplanted to the north, I didn't notice Anne right away. She just blended in with the newness of it all. But gradually she began to emerge. Without any effort, we found ourselves sharing a chemistry lab, a music folder in choir, lunch in the cafeteria. We fell in step naturally. I opened myself willingly. No hesitation. No sizing up the risk. No fear of losing.

The pieces that made up Anne's character sometimes were revealed in surprising ways. One day at lunchtime in the noisy cafeteria, just before Anne was to leave on a two-week tour of Europe with her family, someone brought up the subject of God. "I figure it this way." Renée was speaking. She and Anne had been babies together and were a breed of life-long friends you don't see very often. "This world is in too big a mess for there to be any God of love and order. If He made us, He's sure forgotten us. So why should I remember Him?"

I almost suffocated on my mouthful of crackers. I had to jump in. But Anne was there before me. "That makes about as much sense as tearing the Thomas Edison pages out of the encyclopedia just because we don't understand how electricity works." No one could think of a comeback. Anne had the final word.

Smart answer. Wonder what Anne believes. Must remember to bring up the subject when she gets back from Europe.

"Ready to go?" Anne's voice brought me back to the present. "We get to the scenic part soon. You haven't seen anything yet." With one light spring, she was in the saddle ready to go. I followed with much less grace and precision. *Which goes to show, it pays to start riding when you're three,* I thought to myself as I turned Brighton northward for the second lap of the trip.

It seemed to me that the horses were in stocking feet. Their hooves padded softly on the packed dirt. The tranquillity of these wooded foothills should never be disturbed, I decided. There was no need to clutter the peacefulness with talk. Apparently Anne felt the same way. We rode on to the beat of horseshoes, the scattered symphony of birds overhead, and an occasional rustle of leaves when a ground creature scurried for cover.

Anne was a calm, easy feeling for me; if I didn't feel like talking, I didn't have to say something just to be polite. In the year and a half that I had known her we had done a lot of talking, but we didn't have to fill every moment with conversation. Sometimes, like right now, it took silence to enjoy the beauty. Anne understood that—another reason why I liked being with her.

Sometimes I felt strange about my growing fondness for Anne. A gnawing premonition lodged somewhere in my brain that something hung over our friendship, like a giant scissors waiting for the appropriate moment to cut our togetherness in two. I didn't understand my fears.

Maybe I was afraid of my reasons for being Anne's friend. There were plenty of fringe benefits: a free, open-ended pass to her Olympic-size swimming pool nestled on the brow of one of our town's finer hills; tennis anytime on the immaculately groomed courts that overlooked a terraced garden and patio; quarter horses at the stables; and tickets to parades as a passenger in one of the fifty antique cars her dad owned and showed all over the country.

But our friendship had begun long before I knew about the bonuses. I was convinced that this relationship was not built on the fringes, especially since that memorable evening last spring, almost a year after we'd moved to town. . . .

We'd just finished hitting some tennis balls. Anne was coaching me on some beginning strokes. She was almost as much a pro at tennis as she was at horsemanship. She and her dad had lined their downstairs recreation room with their trophies. Anyway, that evening we were worn out from chasing balls and were reviving ourselves with lemonade on the patio, when Anne brought up the topic of faith.

We'd talked about Christianity before. In fact, Anne had even started going with me to an early morning Bible study some of the kids held in a home near school. She had an expandable index in her brain for filing new information—especially when it came to Christianity.

Sometimes I understood her questions; sometimes I didn't. Sometimes I knew the answers; sometimes I had to go home and ask my dad. Anne and I were learning together. The only difference was that I had accepted the basic premise of Christianity—that God and I were alienated and that Christ was the only one who could bring us together—and Anne was still asking questions, not only about the basic steps, but about issues that the religious professionals had been debating for years. Anne stimulated me by her investigation into God.

The culmination of her quest came without great waves of

emotion. Between sips of lemonade she said simply, "I've decided to trust God with my life." She made little circles in her crushed ice with the end of her straw. "It makes a lot of sense to let the One who created you run your life for you. The job is too big for me anyhow. I think I really do need His help. Guess I should go ahead and tell Him so, huh?"

Anne prayed with her eyes open while she braided her straw, and afterward she apologized for her lack of polish at prayer. "It's the first time I've ever talked to God out loud except to say grace at the table. Forgive me if it sounded kind of awkward." Anne's effort had been sincere. That was all that mattered to me. I felt that it was the start of a new adventure for Anne and me together—a unique bonding that drew us even closer. I was optimistic about our future. . . .

Anne's voice broke my reverie. "See that hole in the hill over there? They call it Marner's cave. They named it in honor of Silas Marner, the one who hoarded all his wealth." Anne turned her reins slightly to the left to avoid an overhanging branch. "Author George Eliot. Remember tenth grade literature, or didn't you read it? Anyhow, legend has it they found shoe boxes stuffed with hundred-dollar bills and an old hermit living here some fifty years ago. Who knows? It makes a good story anyhow." I had a sudden urge to kick Brighton in the ribs and hurry him along past the cave.

The sun was just above the rim of the foothills as we turned into the clearing that led to the stables. "Riding is the best way I know to clean the cobwebs out of the old brain. Don't you agree?" Anne took the reins of my horse and led him toward the barn. "Monday it's back to the grind. But there will be more Saturdays. Are you up for doing this on a regular basis? Maybe every other week or so? The horses need the exercise, and it's much more fun exercising them when you're along."

I loosely committed myself to Anne's horse exercising program and assured her that I could think of no other way I'd rather spend a Saturday afternoon. In my mind I envisioned many more happy times with Anne on the trail. In fact, right at that moment I felt that the adhesive that held us together was so strong that nothing could come between us. I was soon to find out differently.

"See you Monday in choir." Anne waved to me from the little blue car her dad had given her for her sixteenth birthday. "Today sure was fun," I shouted back. It had been a good day. "Memory days," my mother called them. The kind you remember for years to come. I knew it took a special friend like Anne to make them happen.

"Did you see the new girl?" Anne greeted me Monday morning as I walked into choir. "She's short. Has blond hair and blue eyes. Really cute. All the boys have spotted her. Someone said she's from Connecticut. I saw her as I came past the office. I hope kids are nice to her. You got off easy. I think it was your southern accent that did it."

I made a mental note of the information Anne had given me and resolved to make an extra effort to see to it that the Connecticut transfer did feel at home. I knew what new girls on campus felt like. It was not an easy feeling.

The opportunity to put my welcome plan into action came sooner than I'd expected. She was stranded at the intersection where the science wing joined the main corridor. She looked like a motorist who had just run out of gas. Anne and I were on our way from choir. We both sensed her dilemma.

"Need some help?" We were suddenly committed. I saw it as a temporary commitment—a day or two of showing Beth around, helping her find some friends, a good Samaritan kind of venture.

But when she showed up Tuesday at our early morning Bible study, I got the first clue that this chance meeting in the hallway intersection had far greater implications. "Isn't it neat?" Anne whispered to me as I pulled up a cushion and sat down on the floor beside her. "She's a Christian, too. Let's offer her a ride to school." I had a sudden uneasiness about Anne's enthusiasm. For the first time I felt I had to earn the right to be Anne's friend.

"Friendship is not that way," mother said one day not long after Beth transferred in. "You don't have to prove anything. Just be you. Anne likes you for who you are, not because you're better than someone else. Don't make a contest out of it."

But down inside I felt the competition. It followed me whenever Beth was around, and even when she wasn't—to choir where three of us now shared a folder of music instead of just two; to the tennis court where we played round robin rather than singles; to the corner drugstore where we stopped for ice cream sundaes; and even to Bible study where now I had a prayer group of three rather than a prayer partner.

I was always aware of Beth's presence and of how I was doing in comparison. Anne's friendship was suddenly becoming more and more valuable to me. I thought a lot about the good times of the past. She and I had had something special going. I wondered if she remembered.

"Congratulations." My dad handed me the postcard as I rushed in from school one Thursday afternoon. "We think you'll do a fine job for us," it said. "You can begin work this Saturday. Please bring social security card." Dad watched for my excitement to surface. I'd been waiting for this job for months.

"But, dad, I can't start this Saturday. Anne and I are going riding. We planned it weeks ago. How about Monday after school?" I could tell dad wasn't impressed with the idea. In his usual calm way of tossing the ball back into my court, he said simply, "Depends on how badly you want the job. College isn't free you know." I knew he had the upper edge in the debate.

"That's okay," Anne said brightly. She was wearing her green Pendleton blazer, the one she often wore on the trail. Only today she wore it with the Black-Watch Tartan kilt she'd bought in Scotland. Her dark hair bounced as she talked. "Beth already said she'd like to go with me. Her dad signed her up for lessons at the stables, so Saturday afternoons will be good practice for her. I'll have plenty of company." She seemed to be looking right past me as she talked.

I felt like I'd just been crowded off the trail—thrown from the saddle. I knew that I'd never be able to afford riding lessons. Beth had won another round.

That Saturday afternoon I learned to operate a cash register and to twirl rotating racks of dry cleaning. But my mind was on the trail, pushing through the silent green screen of forest, watching chipmunks scurry for cover, sipping hot chocolate from a thermos, galloping full speed across open meadows, having a friend say, "It's always more fun when you're along." Only this time someone else was in the saddle.

I knew there would be more afternoons like that for Anne and Beth. I'd seen it coming and had begun my withdrawal—at least physically. Emotional withdrawal was another matter.

Today, however, as I punched cash register keys and counted change, there was a dull ache deep in my stomach. Things had been so happy before the competition. Safe. Secure. Non-threatening. I'd never even thought of losing—didn't really think I had anything to lose. But all that had changed now. Now there was a third party. Transferred loyalty. Contest lost. The agony of defeat. You don't forget defeat. Its taste lingers.

Time teaches you to fear being crowded out again. Next time, a threesome becomes an uncomfortable contest. Human chess-players vie with one another. Friendship is reduced to a kind of Parker Brothers game you play. When there are more than two, someone must lose. That's how it was last time. And since the loser happened to be you, you play the next round even harder. Your mind becomes a giant scoreboard of wins and losses, haves and have nots, cans and cannots, opponents competing for your circle of warmth.

And in your competitiveness you become protective of the victories you've already scored, jealously guarding the people you love. Cozy partners. Only two. Exclusive rights. Keep it that way. Play the game to make sure you do. Otherwise someone else might grab your friend's attention, steal her affections, win her approval, score higher with her than you do.

But games eat away at genuineness. After a while your friendship becomes no more than a strategy to insure that you win. You make yourself someone you are not—someone you think will score points with your friend. Your uniqueness is diminished by your desire to win—to keep. You've created an artificial preservative for oneness. And so you sit out your winter of competition wearing someone else's form, keeping score, being suspicious of third persons, until in some later season when the trees give birth to growth you learn to put your game boards away and be yourself.

Cancel
the Honors

"Beat you to the top," was the only invitation I needed to race. I dug my toes into the sandy beach and the contest was on—down the little footpath that hugged the coastline, then upward over the boulders of chalk and limestone that made up the white cliffs of Dover.

The channel below us was turbulent. "Pretty good indication there's a storm at sea," the old fisherman had told us earlier that morning as he cranked up his motorlaunch and prepared to head for the deep—out where the Dover sole and herring swam in profusion.

"Angry waters these are sometimes. On days when all I do is work the waves, I say the old Atlantic and the North Sea are at it again. Fighting waters. The two meet in this channel, you know. Then again, some days the waters are friends. Makes for much easier fishing."

I watched him navigate the crescendos of foam with a calm yet rugged control. Tough job. Yet he seemed a tender man. Tough and tender. I liked the combination I saw in the old fisherman.

"What a way to earn a living," I mumbled to Elaine as we

turned down the beach toward the cliffs. The old fisherman's catch would end up in a fish and chips shop in Windsor, some fifty miles north and west. "I landed this contract just after the war and have been serving them ever since," he'd told us.

The limestone slope in front of me was becoming more abrupt. I had visions of being sabotaged by sliding stone and of joining the turbulence of Atlantic Ocean and North Sea below me. Elaine scrambled from rock to rock with the lightness of a mountain goat. She had definitely claimed the lead. I shifted my concentration from winning to maintaining some form of uprightness.

"Truce," I yelled up through the thin air. Judging from the tightness in my lungs, the air was getting thinner all the time. "You win. How 'bout a leisurely walk going down?" Elaine turned around, and I saw her front for the first time in a while. But then, having Elaine out in front was no new experience for me.

Ever since Elaine and I found each other in the registration line our freshman year at the university, we had merged into a strange combination of hierarchy and equality—two individuals who liked to excel, to succeed. But we enjoyed each other in the process. I never thought it mattered who climbed the highest or the quickest. It was just a game we played now and then—friendly competition. At least that's how it seemed.

Maybe we both felt that we'd met our match when we met each other. At any rate, I respected Elaine greatly for her discipline and drive. I felt the respect was mutual. Our Christianity was a common denominator that usually helped us with our competitive balancing act.

"The first shall be last. . . . Whoever wishes to be great shall be your servant. . . ." We talked about Christ's perspective one night as we discussed the "winning isn't everything, it's the only thing" attitude that dominated our campus—a university with no pretense of Christianity.

"Ready to race the channel now?" Elaine made the descent to stand beside me. "Only twenty-one miles to Calais—a mere eleven-hour swim if we were in shape. But since we're not. . . ."

I looked across the expanse. The view was definitely worth the climb.

"The Continent," I mused to Elaine. "Tomorrow we'll see it up close." I shivered. Maybe because the breezes up high were chilly or maybe from sheer anticipation. The Continent was like an unread book to me—shrouded in mystery and antiquity.

"Come on. Let's run. Race you back." Elaine had already started down. Her propensity toward contests was beginning to bother me, especially when the running match was likely to send me hurtling down a slope jutted with sharp protrusions of chalk and limestone.

I declined the race and began to carefully pick my way down along the path of least resistance, a much more sane and scenic way to take the cliffs I'd decided by the time I joined Elaine at the bottom. I complimented her on her speed and agility anyhow. I knew her years of high school track and cheerleading didn't hurt when it came to challenges like the cliffs of Dover.

Elaine was definitely the more athletic of the two of us. "That's probably good," I said to her one day after a freshman-sophomore intramural volleyball game in which we represented both ends of the scoring spectrum. "That way we don't compete, and we can still enjoy the game." Little did I realize that the ultimate contest was yet to come, much farther down the road.

Later that afternoon I shifted the 1,086 pages of *The Norton Anthology of English Literature* to make room for my four o'clock tea and crumpets that Margaret, our thoroughly British hostess, had brought to the garden for us. "How's a person supposed to concentrate on *Beowulf* with all these delicious distractions?" I asked no one in particular. Bogged down in Old English poetry with its unrhymed verse and laborious series of alliterations was not exactly my idea of the best way to spend a sunny afternoon during the first week of our stay in merry old England. I was grateful that we'd at least had the morning to run the cliffs.

Now I had some two hundred pages of introduction to cover in the three days before classes began at the university. Thank goodness nothing much happened in English literature during the six hundred years between *Beowulf* and Chaucer. I counted myself lucky that *Beowulf* was written anonymously. No long, dry historical author data to wade through.

I took a prolonged sip of the liquid mixture before me—a careful blend of light and dark, sweet and bitter. *The English do know how to make their tea,* I thought. Then I picked up my oversized literature book and plunged back in.

Elaine was sprawled in the shade of the high brick fence surrounding our garden. We were in our own little world—walled in by the luxuriance of climbing hybrid tea roses, cape jasmine and rambling English ivy. She'd already finished *Beowulf* and was half-way through Chaucer. I had slim hopes of catching up.

"Don't get bogged down in the details," she said as we jostled down the narrow road from London to Folkestone in a skinny, double-decker bus that leaned precariously into the curves. She showed me the index-card technique. "Keeps your eyes focused on the line, not the words. It'll double your speed."

It came as no surprise to me that Elaine breezed through *Beowulf* in less than half the time it took me. She cranked out a five-page structural analysis of epic poetry while we waited at the airport for our Heathrow to London motorcoach to arrive; she had her first assignment out of the way and we hadn't even left the airport. The ink on our embarkation stamp was still wet.

But that was Elaine—a whiz when it came to the mechanics of the English language and a library on two feet when it came to English literature. It was no secret that all her basic introductory English courses had been waived and that she had moved right into upper division classes her freshman year at the university. There was a certain security about having her as a friend, especially while being on native soil during a six-week crash course in English literature.

Usually Elaine's brilliance didn't bother me, except now and then before a big test when I'd fog through the night on No-Doz and black coffee while she went peacefully to sleep at 10:30 and still pulled a grade above me. Sometimes her excellence was hard to take; but more often I thought of her in terms of having made the big leagues while I was still playing the farm teams, especially when it came to grades.

Sometimes the comparisons were not so easily dealt with, however. Like the day I received official notice from the chancellor's office that I'd been chosen as the sophomore representative for the Chancellor's Senate—an honor not to be taken lightly. I handed the letter with the embossed gold university seal on it to Elaine.

"Well, there's no reason why we can't both be good." Elaine's response had come unchecked. Suddenly I felt there was a part of her I didn't know or understand. Was she joking, trying to convince herself of something? Was she referring to the one-thousand dollar English scholarship she'd received from the university just two weeks earlier? Or was she merely saying congratulations in an indirect sort of way?

"You'll do a good job." Elaine finally caught on that this needed to be my moment of glory. "God can use you in that spot. What an opportunity." Relief. Then she did understand after all. That was the bonus of having a Christian friend on an anything-but-Christian campus. She, too, tried to look at events from God's point of view; and what's more, she could rejoice with me in my successes.

I was sure that Elaine had no idea how much I needed her support right at that moment, even more than I'd needed it on days of defeat. To sincerely support a friend who wins, I decided, was a much truer test of friendship than to stand with a loser. I thanked God for a friend who could celebrate my victories with me.

Meanwhile, *Beowulf*, Chaucer, and the English Channel made sophomore victory celebrations seem long ago and far away. Today was England, fresh and fascinating, full of opportunities to learn. The next six weeks would be like a series of film clips—images, scenes, and information—fed through the projector of my mind at high speed. If the going got tough, I knew I had Elaine to lean on. She could recite the facts and fiction of English literary chronology to me without a moment's hesitation. Elaine didn't miss a fact when it came to the English and their literature. She knew who wrote what, where, when, and under what conditions.

If literature seemed dull to me before, Elaine polished it up for me by filling me in on the details of real-life English drama. I was convinced she was destined for some brilliant English professorship somewhere, sometime.

As for me, there were times when I thought my brain could not absorb one more concentrated dose of rhymed couplets, iambic pentameter, or quatrain stanzas. Then Elaine would suggest biking in the country or catching the train for London. An amazing restoration of tired brain cells took place in London's Westminster Cathedral or as our bikes followed the narrow, winding country roads through patchworks of green, bordered by hedges or stone fences, and dotted with sheep. John Milton's *Areopagitica* went down much easier when digested with a picnic lunch of shepherd's pie and orange squash eaten on a grassy slope that rolled gently into the Thames River.

"Can't let studies interfere with a good time," Elaine said one day as we repacked our books in the knapsack and headed back to the university. Elaine and I were both pretty adept at rationalizing play. But Elaine could afford it. If anyone's studies suffered from a good time, they were mine. It never seemed to make any difference with Elaine.

Unit I was over. We tied the loose ends of the sixteenth century together with a day's trip to Stratford-on-Avon. "This is what I call the bitter with the sweet," Elaine observed as our red motorcoach chugged mildly along the secluded country road that followed the Avon River into Stratford. "Tour today. Test tomorrow. Ayre knows how to plan it right." She referred to our professor who arrived for class every day in a wool tweed blazer and a black bowler hat—the perfect stereotype of a proper English gentleman. "All he needs is a black umbrella," I'd whispered to Elaine after our introduction to him.

Stratford-on-Avon was all the books said it would be. Quaint. Peaceful. Tucked away in a green valley beside the river. "Hey, when did you get to be such an expert on Shakespeare?" Elaine teased as we walked around the Shakespearean characters of bronze in the Bancroft Gardens. I was rehearsing my notes for tomorrow's test as I pointed to each of the aged statues: "Falstaff from *Henry IV*, Part I probably first performed in 1597, first published in 1598; Part II probably first performed in 1598, first published in 1600; Lady Macbeth from *Macbeth*, first performed in 1606, first published in 1623."

Elaine gave me a funny kind of look that made me forget to finish my exhibition of knowledge. "You're going to outshine your faithful, loyal English literature tutor one of these days. That would be like teaching someone to play a new game and then having them beat you. Maybe they should have given *you* the English scholarship."

I wanted to believe Elaine was teasing, but the interior of her words had a cutting ring. We both pretended she didn't really mean it. I mumbled something about the day I won an English scholarship being the day it snowed bananas. But I felt like I had just had my hands slapped for being good—like I had to apologize to Elaine for knowing Shakespeare.

The garden figures faded in significance. I tried to assign some meaning to Elaine's words. True, it had been an exhausting three weeks for us both so far: up early to classes; papers, tests, and reading till late into the night; blitzing the towns and villages of England and Scotland during weekends; and gobbling up as many experiences as possible on foreign soil—collecting both souvenirs and memories to take home with us. But there had to be more to Elaine's comments than that.

True, I had done unusually well on the two quizzes we'd had, and I'd received some high words of praise from Dr. Ayre on the written assignments I'd turned in. But Elaine and I both knew that English literature was her domain. Was she suddenly afraid I was infiltrating her territory? Was that the problem? I wasn't at all sure how I was going to pull back on this one, or even if I should. I could not be untrue to my best efforts. I began to feel the strain on our friendship. There'd been strain before, sometimes caused by who received what letters from back home or who was asked out to dinner. But we'd been honest about those tensions—at least I thought we had. Uusally we ended up praying together about it. I had the uneasy feeling that this time was different.

We continued our tour of Stratford, and the day seemed flawless. But low on the horizon I sensed an ominous and threatening cloud. I couldn't dismiss our garden exchange at Stratford as trivial. In fact, by the time the day was over I was calculating my every word and move. I suddenly felt like I'd been ·dragged into a tournament, whether I wanted to be there or not.

That night I dropped into bed praying that this too would pass—that the contest would end. I was too exhausted to even think about tomorrow's 8:00 A.M. exam.

"Miss Hollinger, may I see you after class?" Dr. Ayre looked down on me from behind his black-rimmed glasses one day about a week and a half after our trip to Stratford. I scrutinized his tone. Good news or bad? I couldn't tell.

"Miss Hollinger," Dr. Ayre began again after class was over. His crisp English accent barely allowed him to pronounce the *H* at the beginning of my name. "I felt it only proper for you to know first. Your piece "Ode to an English Gentleman" was chosen to represent this class at the King Arthur's Festival. It will be listed in this evening's campus news. You may check with the theater department regarding the details of your performance. Jolly well-written piece. The honor was due it."

I sensed a strange ambivalence as I left Dr. Ayre, crossed the gray stone bridge, and headed back toward the residence hall. I'd written the piece in fun—an imitation of the eighteenth century and Alexander Pope. It was meant to express my congenial sentiments toward the English people rather than to win a contest. However, the King Arthur's Festival was an annual event—an exhibition of English literature in both past and present forms—and all English literature students were required to be in competition for it. I'd assumed that my reward would be simply the experience of composing. Elaine's brilliant essay on death and immorality, also in the tradition of Restoration literature, had a much better chance of taking honors, I thought.

Now what? Now that I'd won? Not only had I won a contest; I'd beaten Elaine. A strange kind of fear gnawed at my exuberance and made it something less. What happens to friendship in the strain of competition? What happens to your friend when you come out on top, even when you didn't plan it that way?

I was soon to find out.

Elaine's room was empty when I pushed open her door on my way home from class. She'd been there. Her books were strewn all over her bed. She was still out when I dropped by at four o'clock on my way home from the library. *Strange. Wonder where she is.* I couldn't spend much time trying to find out, with ten pages of typing and one hundred pages of Johnson, Boswell, and Goldsmith to read before bedtime.

A white note card was on my desk when I got back from breakfast next morning. "Thanks for letting me know you won the contest. It was the least you could have done for a friend. Elaine."

That afternoon I went for a bike ride in the country, alone. Elaine excused herself with "too much to do." I was hoping that a quiet talk down by the river might begin the restoration. Elaine never gave me the opportunity.

We spent the remaining two weeks of our study tour on opposite sides of a chasm that grew deeper every day. Words were cold and abrupt—nothing outwardly hostile, but an inner separation of spirit. I reached out into the cold and felt its sting more intensely. After a certain amount of exposure to the frost, you don't venture out any more. After a while I simply stayed inside myself when events forced Elaine and me together.

We had planned to travel home together via Amsterdam for a three-day look at Holland. Now Elaine needed to get home in a hurry. She booked a flight to New York that departed two hours after our last class ended. I took a later flight.

"There's no reason why we can't both be good," Elaine had said long ago in one of our happier times together. Evidently she hadn't really believed it. Right now I wasn't sure that I did either. Can friendship support two people at their best in similar efforts? The answer appeared to be no.

I watched the rolling, green English patchwork slip away from me as the wide-bodied jet roared toward home. *Symbolic*, I thought, *of the friendship I'm leaving behind—drowned by the innocent pressures of a contest.*

Through the years you learn that in avoiding the consequences of a contest you settle for mediocrity. You give, not your worst, lest others reject your indifference, nor your best, lest they be threatened by your excellence. It's better to strike the ordinary course and keep your friend. Don't acknowledge your victories. Pretend they don't exist. Making others aware of your strengths will only remind them of their weaknesses. Don't invite anyone to your celebration of success. In fact, don't even celebrate. A friend may misunderstand your motives. Instead, stifle anything that might surpass another. Keep your gifts hidden. If a friend hands you a bouquet, give it back. Explain that you're really not that good—you just happened to have a lucky break this time. That way a friend won't be uncomfortable or think you're trying to outdo her. It's much easier for someone to identify with your failure than with your success. So in your vulnerability, you expose your weaknesses but camouflage your strengths. A threatened friend is not around for long. To keep your friend, you must not run the risk of intimidating her. For intimacy cannot withstand intimidation.

And so you sit out the winter in the pretense of mediocrity—afraid of outdistancing. Outdoing. Surpassing. Afraid of what your challenge might do to your relationship with your friend. You hold back for the sake of another, convinced that your strengths will create distance rather than bring you together. In the process, you destroy your opportunity for strength as well as your friend's opportunity to celebrate your accomplishment. And on the days when you feel stifled under the lid of another's mediocrity, you imagine a friend who will not only throw a party to honor you, but who will also draw out your dormant abilities and help you become a person worthy of the celebration. You live with dormancy until you learn to honor yourself and begin to bloom again.

Where the
Heart Leads

Time, I thought, is like this giant water wheel, spitting out my life in increments: days, weeks, months, years. Changing forms, yet flowing over a cycle of sameness. Friends come and gone. Hurts harbored and healed. Scenes preserved and discarded. Love lost and found. God, surprising and changeless. But always the desire, like a revolving wheel churning through time, for warmth, for understanding, for acceptance. To know and to be known. To nurture and to be nurtured. To celebrate another's personhood and to be celebrated for your own.

A water wheel. Crude. Simple. But a symbol to me, nevertheless, of the changes in my life over the years. Change of name. Change of address. Change of date. Growth. New sprouts. Tender leaves. Inside and outside transformations. The modulations of my life were reflected back to me in the old miller's stream that rushed over the wheel, then calmed itself and meandered on, out through the Blue Ridge Mountains.

Tomorrow there would be more changes: from play to work, summer to fall, vacationer to student-employee. Life would continue its flow for Mark and me, through the geometric concrete of a cosmopolitan campus and into the routine of graduate students, research assistant, minister, and more important than all the rest put together, partners in marriage. I gave a spontaneous squeeze to the tall, sun-tanned man at my side who was absorbed in silent reverie coming from who knows where. The woodsy enchantment of the old stone mill was broken. We climbed into our car and headed north and west through the mountains, grateful for togetherness, for love, and for God's refreshing creation. Little did I realize that time was soon to test my perspective on all three.

Pen. Paper. Text. Class schedule. Train pass. Lunch. I took mental inventory of my needs for the day, kissed Mark good-bye, and streamlined myself out the door, through the local early morning traffic, and into the station just in time to make the 7:37 commuter to the city—much too close for a comfortable start of the day. *Out of the swing of things. Have to get myself back on schedule. Too much lying around in the sun.*

I was going to miss Mark's companionship in this early-morning routine. Commuting together had been our tradition since he had started graduate work at the university and I'd decided to pick up a few additional courses as well. But this quarter his classes didn't begin until noon; and since I had to be behind my typewriter at the speech research lab by one o'clock, the best I could hope for was a glimpse of him across campus. With as many as 14,000 bodies doing the twelve o'clock shuffle across campus, even the chance of a glimpse of him was awfully slim.

"Psychological Foundations of Communication Theory. Graduate Level." The course description in the catalog sounded interesting enough, but I'd been at the educational game long enough to know that it was the professor who made the class. I knew nothing of Dr. Stacey, except that she had two Ph.D.'s behind her name. I wasn't sure if two Ph.D.'s attached to a professor's pedigree were an asset or a liability to a group of novice graduate students, but I decided it was worth the gamble.

We weren't more than thirty minutes into the first hour lecture when I knew I'd made the right choice. Dr. Stacey was clear, concise, credible, and as authentically academic as any textbook I'd ever read. Not only was she a knowledgeable animated lecturer, but she also came across as a very classy lady. Her brown attaché case had a bold "Ski Breckenridge" tag around its handle, and around her neck on a silver chain hung the only pair of sterling silver skis I'd ever seen. There was no doubt about where she spent her spare time.

Dr. Stacey wasn't the only thing about the class that impressed me. I liked the group, even in its original, undigested form. There were twelve of us in all, and we sat around in an intimate circle, broken only by Dr. Stacey and her blackboard. She didn't need a lectern for her notes; her notes were all in her head. The class would be half lecture, half lab; our only grade would be a group research project to be developed on our own time. I saw hours of extra work, but I also saw possibilities for new ideas and new friendships. There was something stimulating and intriguing about the group around me—a kind of sophisticated mystique that made me want to know more about them. Another five minutes and the opportunity came.

"Senter, Stein, Swansen, and White. Group number four." Dr. Stacey lumped us together into working categories. She handed us each a list. "Ten topic proposals. Choose one. Five-page proposal rationale due Friday. Completed project due November 28. That's it for today." She moved toward the door and left us to our get-acquainted game. We had to find each other. *Smart lady,* I thought to myself as I began the process of elimination. *Let's see. Who looks like a Stein? Thank goodness this is not a class of fifty.*

"Anyone here belong with Stein?" A voice boomed out from over near the door. Instant group. I looked to see who owned the voice. "Your name's not Frank N. is it?" I surprised myself with my lack of inhibition as I moved toward him. It was one way to break the ice.

Stein obviously was used to having his name played with, but he laughed anyhow, like he'd never heard the line before. I noticed that when he smiled his eyes narrowed into an almost straight line. His smile took up all the rest of his face. It was a handsome, friendly face—warm and comfortable. I felt immediately at home. "No, as a matter of fact it's not Frank; it's Rick."

He reached out, shook hands with the other male member of

the group, and completed the introductions. "Now, when shall we meet? Friday comes in four days. Guess we'd best start tracking." He didn't usurp the leadership but seemed to pick it up because it was the natural thing for him to do. We automatically directed our conversation to him.

Going to be an interesting quarter, I thought as I headed toward the south end of the campus, *with the interesting assortment of personalities that make up group number four*. Beth wore an oversize Mickey Mouse wrist watch, smiled very little, and kept referring to the group as "you" rather than "we;" and blond, ruddy-faced Peter from Sweden spoke English in slow, fractured monosyllables, rounded off his w's into v's, and sounded thoroughly academic. Then there was Rick. Casual. Cool. Rugged. Good-looking. Some mother's all-American dream son. I could picture him hoisting the sails aloft amid sparkling blue waters on some TV commercial for aftershave. He had that kind of smile.

Actually I wasn't too far off on Rick's professional expertise. "Into TV production over at channel —." He mentioned one of the larger stations in our city. "I'm here at the station's expense. Hammering away a little at a time on my master's degree in broadcasting."

It was organization time for group number four over at the Pier Room. We discussed project strategy between bites of pizza and the sound of the wailing steel guitars of the current campus "rockers" who provided lunchtime entertainment while they waited to be discovered. I noticed that Rick had outlined the meeting in neat, block printing on a yellow note pad. He'd written his day's schedule in an opposite column. I couldn't miss it. It was right next to my elbow. Besides, organizational ability is one thing I never overlook in people.

"Noon—meet group
2:30—to studio—tape forum
7:30—Bible study at Lynn's."

I almost forgot my manners and charged right into the middle of the conversation. One didn't happen upon another Christian every day on this vast, impersonal commuter campus. Restraint came hard, but I managed to stick to the business at hand until we adjourned the meeting with plans to meet next time at Rick's apartment, which was only three blocks from campus. There we would be able to at least hear each other.

"Hey! Hey! What do you know?" Rick pounded delightedly on the table when I told him I studied the Bible too and, in fact, was personally related to the One who inspired it.

"Now, this is what I call a pleasant surprise." His enthusiasm was obvious. Wait till I tell Lynn. Another Christian—not only in my class, but on the very same team. Lynn's my fiancée. She'll be my wife as of June 27. She's the one who introduced me to Jesus. He was a new idea to me—I'm Jewish. I never knew what I was missing. Making up for lost time now. That's why we started a Bible study. Sixteen came last week. Gee, there's a lot to the Bible. Great learning. I've been a Christian almost a year now, and what a difference!"

"What's changed for you?" I opened the door wide. Forty-five minutes later when I looked at my watch, I realized I was twenty minutes late for speech lab.

"I'll walk you down there. I have to catch the el on South Halsted anyhow," Rick volunteered as I pushed my books into a pile and let him help me with my jacket. It seemed the perfectly natural thing to do.

"Christian friends just aren't that easy for me to come by, especially ones like you who've had a lot more time to grow." He invited Mark and me to his Bible study and promised that sometime he would show me some of the poetry he'd written since becoming a Christian. "See you tomorrow." I felt his smile go right inside me. It was penetrating. I watched him as he jogged across the street and toward the el platform. Smooth. Easy. Muscular form. I felt his magnetism.

"Pleasant surprise," he'd said. I could see why he'd probably be good at writing poetry. It *was* a pleasant surprise to find someone who knew and understood and shared the value of your faith. Almost like finding a long-lost cousin. Instant ties. A prefabricated backdrop to another's life that you don't have to fill in. You just know certain things about that person even without going into all the details. I felt like I'd known Rick for a long time. *That's what*

Christian friendship is all about, I thought to myself as I bounced up the stairs and unlocked the door to apartment 2-B.

"Guess what." I dropped my books on the dining room table and swung into Mark's arms. "Remember the Rick I told you about—the rough and ready, good-looking one? He's a Christian. I read his schedule for the day and saw 'Bible study' written on it. He and his fiancée lead one. He invited us. I told him we had one of our own tonight. You must meet him. You two would hit it off. He's into TV production over at channel —."

Mark grinned and kissed me on the nose. He knew the value of friendship, especially friendships that extended us beyond our present parameters. Over the years since our marriage our lives, individually and as a couple, had formed various combinations with other people. But once in a while friends came along with whom there was a special blend. Mark and I both knew that regardless of which of us was a part of the initial blend, the other would cash in on the dividends of that friendship as well. I sensed that Rick would be no exception.

When it came to Lynn, I wasn't sure. She appeared on the scene the following day at Rick's apartment. The "Psych Foundation's Foursome," as Rick called us, was huddled around his glass-topped, tree-trunk-turned-coffee-table putting the last-minute alterations on our project proposal when she pushed open the apartment door. I would not have guessed she was Lynn except by deduction. *What other female would be pushing open Rick's door in the middle of the afternoon?* The surprise was that she didn't fit my expectations for the woman Rick would choose.

A shy smile played around her mouth and tried to come out. Rick jumped to her rescue and made the introductions. She wore white and had just come from instructing nurses down at the medical center. I was sure that with her street clothes on she'd look much more colorful and interesting. *Probably just what Rick needs— calm, quiet stability and inner strength.* But the outward contrasts in their personalities were striking. She stayed for a while, refilled our brown coffee mugs, and brought out fresh zucchini nut bread. She moved so quietly in and out of the rooms, I almost forgot she was there.

"Do I have a question for you." Rick made the statement one day several weeks later as he squeezed his tall frame into the desk next to mine. "By the way, you and that color green go great together. You look as luscious as lime sherbet on a hot summer day. Now here's the issue. Someone brought it up in Bible study last night." He didn't give me time to respond to his flattery. But then, that was a part of Rick I never took too seriously. He knew how to make people feel special—everyone and anyone. It had been amazing to watch him soften Beth. Recently she'd even referred to the group as "our group." She almost seemed to be enjoying our meetings, and for certain she enjoyed Rick. But then, who didn't?

Rick leaned toward me and started doodling on his yellow note pad. He seemed to pull his thoughts out of the blank sheet of paper.

"As a Christian, when you make a decision is it you that makes the choice or is it God who runs the controls—regulates your mind to make the choices that are consistent with His will? Put it this way. Do you feel that God leads you to do certain things or does He allow you to make the choices that seem most logical to you? If your choices happen to work in your favor, is it because you made the right decision or is it because you have done the will of God?" He dropped his voice to a whisper. Dr. Stacey had started her lecture. "Do you know what I'm saying?"

I nodded that I did. "Let's talk about it later," I scribbled on my notebook paper. I was glad for the two hours of lecture to think about a response. I'd never thought about God's will in quite the way he was asking about it. This wouldn't be a conversation we'd tie up in five minutes after class.

Dr. Stacey had barely finished her diagram of Osgood's and Tannenbaum's Congruity Theory when Rick leaned over and asked, "How about solving this theological dilemma over a Big Mac? I really need your thoughts on this one, but I have to eat and get to the studio by 1:30. Come on. My treat."

The day was warm for September. I threw my blazer over my shoulders as I followed Rick through the door and into the brilliance of noon—a sharp contrast to two hours of artificial lighting in the pie-shaped concrete wedges that the architect had designed for classrooms. Lucky for me that today was my afternoon off at the speech lab. I'd planned study time in the library, then a three o'clock rendezvous with Mark after his class.

"Too nice a day for inside. Let's get our food and then come back and eat on the triangle." Rick referred to one of the few slabs of green on the whole campus, over by the west entrance. A nice little park, complete with white birch, Austrian pine, and a three-layered fountain. It happened to be one of my favorite spots—an oasis in the stark concrete desert that made up the university. How did Rick know that I liked white birch and Austrian pine? There were plenty of other spots we could have eaten. *Could be he likes the place, too,* I thought to myself as we headed west on Harrison toward the golden arches. *Sometimes people enjoy the same things. That's why it's fun to be with them.* Being with Rick seemed a natural, profitable way to spend a lunch hour, especially when we were discussing the will of God. I had no second thoughts.

The hour flew. With Rick I never had to wonder how to start a conversation or what to say next or even if he'd heard what I just said. Rick gave me 100 percent attention—an affirmation that I didn't overlook. From somewhere over toward the library the 1:05 buzzer reminded us of time. "You've got to go. I don't want to make you late for the studio."

Rick seemed to be in no special hurry as he gathered my lunch wrappings together with his and stuffed them into the empty McDonald's bag. "This has really been helpful, Ruth. Thanks for your time. I wish I knew my Bible the way you do. In fact, you're really into a lot of things. You enjoy life don't you? You're an amazing person." He reached out and gave my arm a little squeeze.

"By the way, when are you going to bring Mark out of hiding and let me meet him? Could I talk the two of you into a Saturday brunch sometime. That's when Lynn and I do a lot of our entertaining. Omelets are my specialty. Check with Mark on a date and let me know."

He swung his brown leather jacket over his left shoulder, picked up his attaché, flashed his wide smile, and was gone. He even remembered to take the empty McDonald's bag with him to deposit along the way.

I sat for a long time, mesmerized by the cascading liquid

sculpture of the fountain and by thoughts of Rick. What was it about him? Was he an open door of friendship to everyone who came along? Did he absorb everyone into his life and thoughts the way he'd done with me? I concluded that Rick knew how to invest himself in people. With him there were no categories. No barriers. Friendship was friendship. He spread it generously.

And then, there was our conversation. I didn't remember ever having had such an invigorating dialogue on the will of God with anyone. Maybe it was his young faith or maybe his authenticity, but Rick had a refreshing way of taking the theoretical and nailing it right down into his world.

"Take my relationship with Lynn, for example," he'd said at one point. "Does God have only Lynn picked out for me to marry, or could I marry someone else and still be in God's will? Should we say that we are getting married because it is God's will for our lives, or is it that, as two Christians in harmony with God's spirit, we are getting married because it seems the logical thing for us to do?" There had been no need for me to answer. Rick had more on his mind.

"Sometimes I worry about that." He leaned back against the legs of a concrete park bench. "What is it that makes two people compatible. If it's God's will, should all the other differences not matter? Lynn and I are about as different as two people can be. But she's good for me; she draws me to God and gives me support and strength. Is that enough? Sometimes I feel like a yo-yo." He looked relieved to have said it.

Hard questions. Don't think he expects easy answers either, I thought as I picked up my books and headed toward the library. *No pressure to deliver God's will to him in five easy installments.* I'd surprised myself with my candor as we talked. Being able to express my own tensions about the will of God and not have someone register disappointment in me or make me feel as though I'd let them down gave me a relaxed, genuine kind of feeling. With Rick I didn't feel the need to have my Christianity all sorted out and stored in neat little properly labeled boxes to be pulled out when the appropriate question was asked. I sensed that he valued order but also understood disarray because he understood life, people, and process. Rick's friendship gave me room to be myself. I was amazed that his Christianity had progressed so far in such a short time.

The will of God came up again a few weeks later—this time over a ham and cheese omelet cooked to perfection. Rick had kept his promise—brunch for four at his apartment. He poured freshly squeezed orange juice into tall glasses, set the basket of croissant rolls on the table, and, with the ease of someone who serves brunch every morning of his life, took his place in the empty chair between Lynn and me.

The dynamics of the morning flowed together with easy, pleasant precision: the sounds of coffee bubbling in the percolator, Handel's *Water Music* in the background, the warmth of splattered sunlight over natural woods, earthtones, and hanging gardens of green. *A delicious taste of friendship,* I thought to myself as I watched Mark reach for another roll and throw his head back in uproarious response to Rick's joke about a rabbi, a priest, and a Southern Baptist preacher. Humor from the same mold. No wonder they enjoyed each other. Rick and Mark were an interesting study in constrasts and similarities. I found myself making mental notes on each.

As for Lynn, she drifted in and out of the conversation—mostly in on topics of spiritual significance. I could tell her commitment to God was deep. She was the one who opened the discussion on God's will, leaning forward in her chair, her folded arms lining the edge of the table, her large, dark eyes dissolving into a mirror of serious concentration when she spoke. She directed her questions to Mark. I wondered what else was inside her besides tough, theological questions. There seemed to be a lot of Lynn under lock and key. *How do I draw it out of her, or would she even give me the chance if I tried.* Rick seemed to surface spontaneously—a much easier incentive for friendship. You couldn't help but get to know someone like Rick. He and Mark talked as though they'd been friends for years.

Our verbal exchanges weaved in and out among topics of Jewishness, theology, television producing, golfing, graduate projects for communictions theory, Dr. Stacey, the will of God, marriage. The rolls and coffee had long since disappeared, the morning turned into noon, and I felt we'd just begun. We said good-bye in the front hallway, right next to Rick's hanging gallery of snapshot memorabilia.

"See you Monday, Ruth," Rick called as we started down the stairs. Suddenly Monday morning became significant. Special. An anticipated event. I checked my enthusiasm for Monday mornings. I had never felt that way before about the beginning of a work week. Could it be I enjoyed Foundations in Communication Theory enough for it to transform Mondays? But then, I'd had stimulating classes on Mondays before. Down deep I knew it had something to do with Rick. After all, who doesn't look forward to being with friends. But attachment to another person always has risks. I knew this time the risks were even higher. I slid over close to Mark and took his hand. I felt a little more secure.

"Going to Houston," Rick boomed out one morning near the end of the quarter as he met me in the hall outside class. "Don't look so shocked. It's only a five-day convention. Be back a week from Friday, just in time for the grand finale to this outstanding production by group number four. I think we can tie it all up when I get back, don't you?"

I was sure we could tie it all up when he got back; but I suddenly felt at loose ends anyhow, like someone had just cut next week out of my calendar. Why should it matter so much that Rick went to Houston next week? The project was in final stages. Research was done. Tabulations were all in, and we were ready to draft our final observations and conclusions. There was no reason why we couldn't proceed without Rick; my head struggled to convince my heart. I rode home on the train that afternoon feeling that life had boomeranged back into the ordinary, at least for next week. But then, it's natural to miss your friends when they're gone. I felt uneasy, just the same, that a convention in Houston could disrupt my happiness.

That night during my conversation with God, I played an edited tape of my feelings. I could not bring myself to verbalize the growing tensions inside me. Surely God understood about friendship. That's why He created companionship for Himself in the garden. But when it came to this particular friendship—the one that drew Rick and me together—I felt God was strangely silent. I'd always assumed the male-female "thou shalt nots" in the Bible were for the extremes. I was walking down the middle of the road with Rick. The guideposts did not seem so obvious.

The call from Houston came on Wednesday afternoon just after I'd gotten home from school. "Just can't get along without me now, can you? Tell the truth." He didn't give me time to tell him, and I wouldn't have anyhow. "Do me a big favor. Peter didn't have his cross-tabs done on the Edgebrook sample. Check with him tomorrow. Dr. Stacey needs to see a copy of the stats, too. Would you get them to her before Friday? Thanks. You're a nice lady. So what's been happening in your life since I've been gone?"

I wasn't sure I understood his question so I told him that the temperature had dropped to fourteen degrees last night—first time in twenty years it'd been this cold so early; that we had finished Festinger and the Cognitive Dissonance Theory in class; and that Mark and I had eaten at the Greektown restaurant he'd recommended to me one day during a conversation about ethnic foods.

Rick seemed to forget that he was calling me from Houston. He described his hotel, the giant American flag that was flying above the hotel portico, the view from his fifteenth story window, the Mexican dinner he'd eaten the night before in Houston's Old Town, and the speech on the future of coaxial television that he'd just heard at the convention.

When it was all over, I sat for a long time and stared at the phone. *A lot of conversation just to tell me about Peter's cross-tabs. Where is this thing going?*

It was a question I didn't want to answer. But I didn't have to, at least not right then. Instead, I felt like singing. And I did. All the way through the rest of the evening. "It's getting near the end of the quarter. You're singing again. You feel out from under the pile, don't you?" Mark made his observation that night at dinner. I couldn't bring myself to tell him any differently. I never mentioned Houston or the call.

Strange that I felt the need to hide a phone call I'd received from a friend. I knew Mark would understand. I'd always basked in the strength of our trust and commitment to each other. Why then the sudden need for secrecy? Mark and I'd never played hide-and-seek games before. It was an uncomfortable procedure—foreign to our way of doing things. But then, maybe there comes a time in marriage when you need privacy. Space. Your own friends. Maybe you reach a point where some details don't need to be joint ownership.

I drifted in and out of a troubled sleep. Images and thoughts of Rick pounded at my mind. Mark seemed far away, even though I could feel his strong, secure body next to mine. Male-female friendships. They'd never troubled me before. This time was different. This time involved my heart. I knew I missed Rick for reasons far deeper than a communications theory research project. His phone call told me how much I cared.

The next four days passed in slow motion. My mind was in Houston. Meanwhile, I carried out the functions of here and now and waited for Monday. Each ring of the phone reminded me that Rick could be at the other end of the line. Maybe he'd forgotten something else about the project. For the first time in our marriage I wondered if Mark ever read my diary. I'd never thought about my need for privacy before. Suddenly, it seemed very real. I'd never consciously measured Mark against another man before. Now the contrasts seemed glaring and not at all in Mark's favor.

Where is this friendship taking me? I couldn't bring myself to consider an answer. I wasn't sure I wanted any messages written in neon lights from God. When something seems so special—so easy and natural, so comfortable and affirming—why spoil it by asking tough questions? Chances are it's not going anywhere other than where it is. It will be what it is now. Why become paranoid about dangers on the other side of the river when you haven't even crossed the bridge?

The minute I saw Rick walk into class on Monday morning I knew this friendship wasn't standing still. No friendship ever does unless it's dead. He'd never looked so good. His rugged, bronzed Houston sun tan was set off by the soft gentle blue in his sweater and in his eyes. It was that mix of tough and tender that I so admired—a rare blend that I didn't find very often in people.

"I had to work in a little golf you know." He swung an imaginary golf club in front of my desk when I asked about getting a sun tan from the inside of a hotel. "Those conventions are hard work. You have to balance it off with some play. Speaking of work—the fearsome foursome has some to do yet."

We agreed that two seven-to-nine evenings at Rick's place should bring us through in time for the Wednesday noon deadline. We had built our investigation carefully and critically. The project would be a monumental accomplishment for us all.

The November night was cool as the wind blew in off the lake. Rick and I walked toward his car—into the wind. I shivered and he offered me his brown leather coat. The project was done and was ready to be delivered to Dr. Stacey's office by noon tomorrow. The final stroke had come at 10:20, just seventeen minutes after the last train west until midnight. Beth and Peter had their cars, but lived south. "I'll run you home," Rick volunteered. "Now that this masterpiece is done, I have all the time in the world." It did seem like a logical solution to my dilemma, but first the four of us walked around the corner for a donut and coffee to congratulate ourselves on a job well-done.

Sliding into the passenger's side of Rick's yellow Datsun 280Z I felt ambiguities similar to those I experienced every time I rode a 747 at thirty-five thousand feet in the air—the excitement of the skies juxtaposed against safe ground beneath me. Why my hesitation? *Friends give each other rides home all the time. Why should this be so different?* Rick and I both seemed to know it was. He verbalized it first.

"Know what, little lady?" His words sounded natural and easy. "I missed you while I was in Houston. I found myself thinking about you a lot." He took a deep breath. I felt my heart racing. "And I'm going to miss you tomorrow when there's no class. I like you. I like you a lot. You are all the things I admire in a woman— all wrapped up in one person. I've never found that before. You understand me better than some who've known me all my life." I saw a look of tenderness on his face that I hadn't seen before. "Ruth, I think I love you."

I felt like the whole inside of me was vibrating. The night was rushing past the headlights, through the windshield, and into my brain. Night. Fog. Clouds. Confusion. A complex jumble of emotions, images, sensations, expectations, rules, and commitments—a bombardment of feelings I didn't even recognize.

Rick broke the silence. "A penny for your thoughts."

My thoughts were coming too fast to unscramble. "It's just— I—well, I—I hadn't planned on this friendship becoming so—so complicated. I thought it would just be a friendship. . . ."

"You can't program your heart, you know." Rick said it so softly it almost sounded like poetry.

"I know. Now I know. Rick, you're a very special person to me." I looked away from him and tried to pull the fragments of my thoughts together. "I love you as a friend—a friend in Christ—I think. I thought I knew the difference between kinds of love—now I'm not so sure. Where *is* the line? How do you know when you've crossed it?"

"We never ask easy questions do we?" His strong, confident hands gripped the steering wheel. There seemed to be something in our dilemma that was drawing us even closer. "Maybe we come right back to the will of God. What is it for you and me? Can't it include our caring for one another, even though we are male and female with other commitments which we honor? If not, what do I do about you? Amputate my emotions? Pretend I never met you? Act as though you are dead?" I heard frustration in his words, saw tension in the lines across his forehead. I wanted to put my arms around him and tell him not to worry, that everything would be okay. But I couldn't tell him it would be okay. I didn't think it would be.

"There are other classes you know." I felt him straining for resolve. "I'll be on campus another two years. Tomorrow doesn't have to end it all. Couldn't I see you now and then? Have lunch here and there—just to keep in touch? Besides, who would understand my wild questions about faith and Christianity? At least, who else would give me permission to ask them?" He smiled at me with his warm, contagious, gentle smile and raised his eyebrows as though waiting for my answer. I never gave him one. At least not then.

"Please smile for me," Rick said as we pulled up in front of my apartment building. "If I never see you again, I don't want to remember you with tears in your eyes."

I felt like my throat was closing off. The possibility of never seeing him again sounded like a deathblow. I wasn't sure I was prepared for it, at least not yet.

"Give you a call sometime," he said. I didn't know whether he meant it as a question or as a statement, so I said only, "Good night, Rick. Thanks for the ride," and slipped out of his car. I hardly had strength to climb the stairs to our apartment—where I knew Mark would be waiting.

"Lord, hang on to me," were the only words I could pray. I knew God would, but I needed to say the words to Him anyhow. They were urgent words that I said more than once in the days that followed, when I felt like I was balancing precariously on the rim of a giant precipice.

"Unto Him who is able to keep you from falling. . . ." I remembered the words of the benediction from the Book of Jude. I felt arms reaching around me. Hugging me. Drawing me close. God's arms. Mark's arms. Strong. Secure. Safe. Loving me. Supporting me. Believing in me.

I knew what I had to do. The courage to do it didn't come overnight. But one day I sat down at my typewriter and typed the letter. I typed it on blue monogrammed notepaper and addressed it to his home. "Friendship is always going somewhere unless it's dead." I'd said it to him before, but I said it again. "You and I both know where ours is going. When a relationship threatens the stability of commitments we've made to the people we value the most, it can no longer be." I folded the letter and watched it disappear down the mailbox chute. There was no way I could get it back now.

I felt that final ripping apart with every part of my body. My hands shook as I typed the letter. My eyes stung. My insides felt like lead. But I also felt the load shift—from my shoulders to God's. I'd obeyed that inner voice. I'd done what I knew I had to do. I would trust God to heal the wounds. The ultimate triumph belonged to Him. I knew myself too well to think otherwise.

But sometimes in the aftermath of our bent toward extreme— when our hearts have led us where our heads would not have led—we learn stoicism. We become passive—we become indifferent to relationships, especially the ones we sense could bring us pleasure. It was joy that misled us and pulled our hearts down a dead-end street; and it was warm affirmation from another that colored our reality and clouded our reason. Once betrayed by emotions, can we trust them again?

And so we become tough disciplinarians of our feelings. We place them under lock and key, allowing brief spurts of spontaneity, but only when it is measurably safe. We cut ourselves off from any potential preoccupation and, in the process, clip ourselves from any relationship that may involve our hearts. "Potential Danger. Keep Away." But after a while we can't tell whether the danger is real or imagined. We put up our own signs, constructed from our memory of what happened last time. We forget about the stronger hands that kept us then.

The winter of our stoicism surrounds us until, in another time and in another place, we learn about balance and about God's provision for keeping His creation on course.

6

Frozen
Reservoirs

We'd played the waves all afternoon—swam them, floated on them, and tunneled them. They'd been friendly waves then, the kind we could run into with open arms. Once in a while, just for fun, we'd let them chase us. Not because we were afraid of them, but because they were a game. The lifeguard's whistle changed everything.

Almost before the sound registered, the rescue specialists were in their life jackets, propelling their craft with powerful strokes right past us and out toward the dark form that was appearing and disappearing in the watery turbulence.

"Everybody out. Out of the water, please. Everyone on shore." The megaphones amplified the message, spreading it up and down the beach. No one disobeyed. We crouched on the sand like a herd of stunned animals—too frightened to watch or to look the other way. There had to be something someone could do. But there wasn't.

Nothing moved. Even the hands on the clock that was nailed to the side of the umbrella and raft rental shack seemed to stand still. Salt hung heavy in the air. The sunlight faded into a strange yellowish palor, almost cadaverous in hue. I wrapped my beach towel tightly around me and shook. Even before the lifeboat came close enough for us to see the gray blanket draped over the motionless cargo on the bottom of the boat, we knew that it was all over for someone. No one knew for whom. We would never know.

The next day there were no visual reminders that a man had drowned here yesterday. The waves washed cleanly in and out. But my mind wouldn't let me forget. I hesitated at the water's edge, felt for the undertow, expecting that at any moment it would grab me and pull me under. I dove through a wave and came up gasping for air, struggling to find a foothold. Invisible suctions sometimes swallowed people whole. I'd seen it happen yesterday. Today I felt its pull, and I struggled physically and mentally to keep myself afloat. I pictured myself going under, and I fought for survival.

That was mid-June, vacation time at the New Jersey shore. Within a couple months, the experience was only a dull memory of stored-away sensations. But years later those sensations were reawakened, and the consequences for me were even greater than they were on that summer day along the Atlantic Ocean. . . .

The train was filled with holiday shoppers. Everyone seemed to have caught the spirit. Usually commuters travel in isolated compartments all their own. No one ever disturbs another's space. Today the walls were down. Strangers met and talked like old friends. Camaraderie was everywhere. The spell of silence was broken by the fact that Christmas was just three days away.

I crushed my bundle of packages together, steadied the cup of expresso I'd just purchased in the station, and slid into the first empty seat I could find. Sitting felt good after the brisk eight-block walk from State Street to the station. I'd barely taken my first sip of coffee when the train jerked to a start. Cutting corners close was not my usual procedure, but today all my extra time had been spent trying to find a seat.

The station walls began to move. The light outside the windows went from black to gray to yellow. The city appeared. Bits and pieces of the whole. Fragments of a moving metropolis. Flashes of steel and concrete, chrome and glass were soon replaced by particles from another world. Debris swirled in the alleys.

Tumbled-down back porches and clogged-up yards. Boarded-up windows and rusted-out junk heaps. *The deterioration of life,* I thought heavily to myself. Wonder what these neighborhoods once looked like. Months later I would remember this train ride and the deterioration of life.

The first thing I noticed about my seat partner was that our tickets bore the same blue stamp. We were headed for the same suburb. The second thing I noticed was that she looked very young. "Are you from—?" I mentioned the town where we lived. She nodded and smiled. Her long, dark hair was pulled up from her face in a stylish sweep. On the ring finger of her left hand was an impressive-looking diamond.

She eyed me with curiosity. "You look familiar. I've seen you before. Didn't you help lead a Bible study once over at —?" She named the community center where we'd met. "I came a couple of times with my friend, Jean. Then another baby came along and, well, you know how they can disrupt routines, especially when he's number four in seven-and-a-half years." She laughed with delicacy and tossed her head lightly. She reminded me of a piece of fine china. She showed no signs of the wear from four small children.

"You come into the city often?" There was something about her that made me think she probably did, but I asked the question anyhow. "As often as I can. I love the city. So does my husband, even though he commutes in every day for work. Sometimes I hop the train and come down to meet him for lunch. Today was my own. Pure pleasure. Last-minute Christmas shopping and lunch at the Walnut Room."

I felt immediately drawn to Ellen. We both liked the city, and the Walnut Room was one of my Christmas favorites. We rode toward the suburbs, but our conversation was back in the city—the restaurants we'd been to, the places we'd shopped, the city schools we'd attended, theaters, museums, downtown politics, special events, and Christmas traditions of State Street. She pulled out the framed ink sketch she'd bought for her husband's Christmas present—a misty black and white image of Chicago's historic Water Tower, the lone structural survivor of the great Chicago fire of 1871.

"When this Christmas crunch is over, let's plan a dinner-on-the-town with our husbands. It's fun to share the city with people who are as excited about it as we are. Those kinds are hard to find in our neighborhood. Most people never get beyond the muggings and murders. Look at all they're missing."

Her enthusiasm was obvious. I agreed that true city fans were hard to find in the suburbs and that we'd probably make a comfortable foursome because of our mutual interests. We exchanged phone numbers with promises to call after the new year. Little did I realize where those calls would lead.

The first one led to a lively German rathskeller just west of the Loop. Bob and Ellen had been there before. Mark and I were game for something new. There was no doubt about its authenticity. Sauerkraut. Wiener schnitzel. Sauerbraten. Streusel Kuchen. Muenster cheese. Waiters with heavy German accents.

"Most of these dishes were created originally by the German people to keep their foods from spoiling." Bob filled us in on some of the lesser-known details as we waited for round one of our dinner. At the same time we listened half-attentively to the accordian band that swirled between tables in brown lederhosen and brightly colored skirts with tight waistbands laced halfway up the front.

Bob did most of the talking, his voice fading in and out among the German folk songs. He had a lot to say about his world-wide travels for a major oil company and his climb toward the pinnacles of corporate management. He built sailboats in the summer and created gourmet dishes whenever Ellen would allow him in the kitchen. He looked at her when he said it.

Once in a while Bob seemed to remember that Ellen was there, but I got the idea that most of the time he was used to soloing. Ellen seemed used to it, too. She sat composed and gracious in her chair like a piece of Royal Doulton china. Occasionally she injected a story or an opinion, but the Ellen of the German restaurant was much more subdued than the Ellen of the pre-Christmas train ride from the city. She watched her husband perform with obvious dedication and affection, laughed at his jokes, and complimented his achievements. When it was time to go, Bob issued a resounding word of congratulations to the band and tipped them generously.

He smiled broadly to the waiters and lifted his hat to the maître d'. His smile showed a perfect set of white teeth. But somehow his smile reminded me of one mysterious day the previous spring when the sun had shone brilliantly on our yard all day, while in a nearby town the storm clouds had rumbled and funneled and wiped out a trailer court. Not until later did I realize the reason for my strange mental analogy. . . .

"Ruth. Could you please come over? I need to talk to you right away." Ellen's voice sounded strangely urgent. I stacked the breakfast dishes in the sink, quickly got my one-year-old ready, and took a deep breath of the fresh June air as I jumped in the car and headed toward Ellen's house. I'd traveled this way so often in the past six months I felt I could make the trip with my eyes closed. Ellen and I had gone back and forth between our two houses for mid-morning coffee together, Bible study once a week, baby-sitting exchange, even a couple trips downtown—just the two of us.

"I really need your friendship," Ellen had said to me one day earlier in the spring as we supervised kids playing in our backyard. "God saved that seat on the train at Christmastime just for you. He knew when the time was right for us to find each other." I sensed Ellen's need—vague and indefinable, yet it locked me to her.

Ellen sounded very emotional that spring morning when we talked about friendship. I was sure she was reacting to the diagnosis from her father's surgery earlier that week—the doctors had found cancer. I was with her when the phone call came from her mother at the hospital. I made dinner for her that night and stayed to help her put the kids to bed because Bob was in Seattle on business. I was sure this morning's call had something to do with her dad. I soon found out differently.

Ellen's house always smelled like a spring bouquet, even in the middle of winter, and her windows always sparkled. This morning was no exception. She had opened the doors and the louvered window shutters to the crisp June day. There was not a fingerprint anywhere, and her coffeepot was plugged in and waiting.

"It's about Bob," she almost whispered his name as we settled down on the patio with our coffee mugs, within full view of the children's sandbox activities. "He's been doing some strange things lately. The kind that happen in soap operas." She took a deep breath as though to find courage to continue. "He hasn't been coming home in time for dinner lately. Says that all of a sudden his work load has gotten heavier. I didn't question his word until yesterday when I discovered that he's had a secret bank account for almost a year now. The bank called me to check out a mistake in interest calculations. He has over five thousand dollars stashed away." She stared blankly at a wooden tub of red and white geraniums.

"Ruth, why has he kept an account for over a year without telling me? Why would a husband do that? I've always gone along with his investments—never opposed his expenditures—never even asked about them. There's always been plenty of money for both of us. I don't understand why. . . ." She took a sip of her black coffee. Her voice drifted off, then returned with force.

"I don't like it, Ruth. Whatever is going on. Things are not normal." She rotated her coffee mug nervously from side to side as though dialing a solution.

"Last night when I asked him about it, he got angry—the angriest I've ever seen him. He accused me of not trusting him, of prying into his personal business, of being a suspicious wife. It didn't seem to matter to him that the bank called *me*, that it wasn't *my* fault I found out. He never even came to bed last night." Her voice faded, and she closed her eyes as though trying to erase the reality. "I guess he slept in the family room. I don't know. He was gone by the time I got up this morning. How do I live with this? It can never be the same. Something has happened."

A door inside her seemed to click shut. I tried desperately to push it back open.

"Ellen, you've got to keep believing in him. He *is* your husband. One leak doesn't have to sink the whole ship." She wasn't looking at me. She hadn't heard. I was losing her. "Ellen," I repeated my words, "you can't afford to stop trusting." This time she looked at me.

"Yes, I guess you're right." But her words were lifeless. I went home that morning feeling that Ellen hadn't heard a word I'd said.

Summer merged into fall, and I was beginning to think that

perhaps the leak had been plugged. Bob admitted he was probably wrong in not sharing his secret savings account with Ellen. But then, a man likes to pursue some business ventures now and then without getting his wife involved in the intricacies of high finance. He'd done it, he claimed, to protect Ellen from all the worry and bother.

Some days Ellen believed him and some days she didn't. "You don't trust the fire once its burned you," she said one day as she replayed the secret bank account experience to me. I'd heard the tape before. Often before. But I listened anyhow.

Some days Ellen's burden seemed light to me. Lately, however, it was beginning to gnaw away at my spirit—at my light-heartedness. The phone calls and conversations with Ellen were becoming more frequent and more urgent. Now it seemed that every coffee time was filled with crises. I found myself longing for a simple, happy conversation with Ellen—the way it had been in the beginning. But my commitment to her had taken us beyond those happy, light times. There was no retreat now. Ellen was too much a part of my time and my thoughts—almost an obsession—like a giant boulder around my neck. I could not dismiss her crises.

"Trust is something someone has to earn," Ellen said one day. "And Bob isn't doing anything to earn that trust any more. How do you trust someone when he works until midnight and always comes home with a new excuse? And I'm supposed to believe in him?"

I detected a calculating tone in Ellen's conversation that hadn't been there before. I'd always enjoyed her spontaneity. Now she seemed to be trying to outdistance her feelings. She'd begun building her wall, I felt, just in case she needed it some day for protection. Suspicion. Fear. Bitterness. Hate. I felt inadequate against her defenses.

Even the long summer days didn't seem to lift Ellen's spirits. Now as fall nipped at the air, I felt like we were walking down a cold, dark tunnel with no light at the end. Tonight even my sleep was troubled—maybe because of a premonition or maybe because Mark and I'd been up doctoring a croupy toddler for the past two nights. When the phone rang, it fit into the flow of disruptions. Our digital clock-radio set the exact moment at 4:07 A.M.

Ellen's voice was faint—like all the life had been drained from it. "Ruth. Bob didn't come home at all last night. I'm worried. I'm scared. What should I do?"

I was still getting dressed as I started the car motor. As I headed down the street toward Ellen's, the neighborhood looked eerie in the interlude between night and day, almost like foreign turf. Probably because I'd never seen it at this hour of the morning. I felt loneliness and fear. I locked all my doors and turned up the radio, not because I feared the neighborhood, but because I feared what lay ahead.

"Lord, I'm not sure I'm ready for this. Teach me how to handle it. We've got to keep this boat afloat, Lord. Please. For Ellen and the kids." The car was cold, but my hands were sweaty against the steering wheel. I wiped them off on my jeans and pressed down on the accelerator. I was racing against something. Trying to keep it from happening. What it was, I wasn't sure. All I knew was I had to get there. I could feel my pulse in my head, the giant boulder around my neck. I had no idea what I would say or do.

It seemed like a night without an end, even though the first slivers of morning were beginning to appear around the slats in the shuttered windows. I could hear the minutes marking time on Ellen's kitchen clock. Ellen was drinking her third cup of coffee. "Just black. I need it black," she said when I poured her fourth cup. I noticed that her hands were already shaking. Caffeine couldn't hurt now. We were waiting. Waiting for anything. The phone. A knock on the door. A car in the driveway. A child to wake up. Anything to break the soundless unknown.

"Where is he? Where's Bob? Where's God while all this is happening? Ruth, what am I going to do?" She cradled her face in her hands. They were delicate hands, not used to hard places. Her pink robe hung limply over her bent shoulders. This morning her whole body looked old. Upstairs one of the children started to cry. I moved quickly and silently to provide comfort. No one else in the house could provide it this morning. It was up to me.

"I'm taking the children with me," I said thirty minutes later when I came downstairs. Ellen hadn't moved from the kitchen table. The only difference was that her coffee cup was empty again. The children were all dressed and ready to go. "Take a shower. Make yourself some breakfast and try to get some sleep. I'll call you at noon to see how you're doing." I felt a new surge of energy. This boat would not sink. At least, not with me on board. I'd said all that needed to be said. Now was the time to act. I was already drawing up plans for Mark and me to sit down and talk with Bob and Ellen together whenever Bob came home. It didn't cross my mind to think, *if* Bob comes home.

Ellen saw me to the door and gave me a hug—baby and all. "What would I do without you, Ruth?" She looked like she was ready to cry again. I wanted to get the children out first. I gathered them quickly through the door and out into the car.

"Where are we going?" four-year-old Jamie asked as he climbed in beside me. I wished I could tell him for sure. But I didn't know, so I simply said, "You're going to my house for a little while."

By noon Bob had called home with a complicated account of meeting a client for dinner, talking until after the last train out for the night, and then sleeping until morning in his office lounge. "I didn't want to frighten you in the middle of the night with a phone call," was the excuse he gave Ellen.

"I've seen this kind of thing in the movies." Ellen's voice was hard. "But I didn't know people, especially my own husband, would be dumb enough to act it out in real life."

Things appeared normal when I took the children home later that evening. Bob met me at the door with his sunny-day smile. "Thanks for taking the kids today and giving Ellen a good break. She needed it. Four kids can be quite a handful. We'll return the favor sometime."

I said good-night and turned toward the car. Nothing else seemed appropriate. The storm was gathering momentum, but there are ways to prepare for storms. I learned about them while living sixty miles inland from the Gulf of Mexico. This time, however, battening down the hatches was beginning to tax my physical and emotional stamina to an extent I'd never dreamed possible.

"You're worried about Ellen, aren't you?" Mark asked gently as we were getting ready for bed one night later that week. "I can tell. You've tossed and turned all night for the last three nights. Back off a little, honey. You're trying to carry the whole load." He sat down on the bed beside me. "Bob and Ellen have to solve their own conflicts. You can't fight their battles for them single-handedly."

I jerked to my feet and fired my words in his direction. "I'm not fighting battles; I'm trying to protect a friend who's being crushed into the ground. And you want me to stand by and watch it happen. Back off! Where do you find that advice in the Bible?" I felt my facial muscles strain and my throat start to vibrate. "When's the last time you had a friend who's given ten years of her life to raise four kids under six—raise them alone, as though they only belong to one parent? When have you had a friend who's made a comfortable, attractive home for someone, entertained his friends and associates, washed his clothes, ironed his shirts, watched him play baseball, listened to him tell his jokes and stories, sat home so he could climb the ladder, only to have him pull out because some-one else is more fun?"

I wanted to scream at Mark—at Bob—at God—at somebody, but instead I said curtly, "And you expect me to stay unaffected?" There was ice in my words but my face was burning. I felt hot all over.

"Wait just a minute." Mark came back on the defensive, his face set like granite now. "Do you know for certain it's because 'someone else is more fun'? I'd advise you not to go jumping to conclusions. Do you have proof to back up a statement like that?"

I heard myself coming on stronger and louder. "I should have expected you to side with Bob. I have a lot more proof than I've told you about." I leaned against the doorframe. I was exhausted, but my discourse was not over. "With all the counseling you've done, you should understand about keeping the confidences of a friend. I have plenty of reasons, but I'm not about to pass them around for public inspection. Ellen has suffered enough without having the sordid details published, especially by her friend."

Mark *leaned forward*—his intensity high, his voice low, his words measured. "I respect your desire to protect your friend. But what I'm saying is that you can't allow someone who is floundering

to pull you down with them. You'll drown yourself in the process."
He reached out for my hand. I pulled away. "That's what I see
happening. You can't solve this one, Ruth. Please stop trying so
hard. You are not the United Nations peacekeeping force."

Mark smiled. He apparently thought his line was humorous. I
turned away. "It's fine for you to be so smug and detached about it
all. We're not talking about your good friend. But I'll not stand by
and see Ellen destroyed. Now, if you don't mind, I'd like to go to
bed. My head is splitting. Would you check on Jori, please?"

I crawled into bed, pulled my pillow over my eyes to keep the
light out, and tried to relax my knotted nerves. *How can he be so cold
and calculating about it all? That's all I need. Tensions in my own house. As
though I don't already have enough with Ellen's.*

I wanted Mark to take me in his arms and hold me. To tell me
everything was safe and secure in our harbor. But I didn't give him
the opportunity. I didn't even know at the time that that was what
I wanted. All I wanted right then was resolution. Something.
Somehow. Somewhere. The burden was beginning to crush me, to
force the breath out of me and my home. It was almost as though I
was living in Ellen's house. Her pain was as real to me as if someone had injected it into my bloodstream. There was no rest in my
sleep.

Winter came again with its cold, harsh winds. They prowled
around the nursery window and came inside and disrupted my
warmth. We rocked late into the night—disquieted mother and
child. Jori. Crying from hurt? Fear? Insecurity? An absentee parent? Three different babysitters in the last two days? She stiffened
her little body against mine, resisting something. I wished I knew
what it was—one more unknown.

Sitting in the darkened nursery with my eyes closed, I hum-
med a little lullaby; but with the wind and the screams, no one
heard, not even me. Singing almost seemed a mockery tonight, but
I did it anyhow—maybe for the symbolism, maybe to remind me of
how things were under normal conditions.

Poignant scenes played themselves out in front of my closed
eyes, almost like someone had turned the projector on automatic
and I didn't know how to turn it off. All the slides were of Ellen.

Ellen. Silhouetted against a train window again, a broken-down city rushing by outside. This time the deterioration had come inside. It was the same city, but a different Ellen. Her eyes didn't smile. Neither did her face. The Ellen I'd met two years ago on that happy Christmas ride from the city didn't live here any more. Her black hair hung straight, and a button was missing from the front of her coat. The diamond was missing from her left ring finger.

We ate at the Walnut Room. *To help us forget, at least for an hour or so,* I thought. It only made us remember. "Bob and I sat at this table once. He liked this place for lunch, especially on Wednesdays when they had the strolling violinists." Ellen wasn't with me. She was with Bob. Somewhere. Sometime in the past. Today lost all significance because today had no Bob in it.

Ellen. At the mercy of cold, impersonal lawyers and judges who fired their questions and made their pronouncements like they were processing paper, not people. Black-robed arbitrators officiating over the death of a marriage. Sharp-tongued referees in the fight for the rites of burial. Ellen sat through the proceedings with her hands holding each other so tightly her knuckles were white. Once I reached over and squeezed them, just to remind her of warmth.

"What did I do to make him hate me, Ruth? Why did he force me to fight him?" She stared pathetically after the tall, immaculately groomed man who walked down the corridor with his lawyer. Ellen and Bob passed each other without a sign of recognition. Total strangers after ten years of marriage. We watched the elevator doors slide shut. We both knew it was over. The final shovel of dirt had been piled in place.

Ellen. The mother of four. Alone in that immaculate house with a nursery and a rocking chair and a baby like mine. Alone tonight with the wind pounding at her windows. Ellen. Ellen. She seemed so far away. So small. So helpless. And I couldn't get to her. I had my own baby in my arms.

I squeezed my eyes shut tightly, but the tears came anyhow. Jori and I cried together. I was awake. Then I was sleeping. Both of us were sleeping. The three of us were sleeping. In my dreams I heard the storm. I felt the waves. Someone was drowning. In panic

I threw the life preserver to them, but the waves got hold of it first and snatched it out of reach. Then I was swimming. Trying to hold on. But the waters grabbed us both, tossed us like corks. I was almost there—almost able to catch on—almost, but not quite. I was going under—under. . . . I lashed out at the dark.

Mark was there beside me. I clung desperately to him. His slow, deep breathing told me he was still asleep. The wind whined outside. I was inside where it was warm and safe. I was safe, but my nightmare hung on; it carried me back to a New Jersey beach one afternoon years ago. I lay awake and stared into the dark for a long, long time.

Morning dawned with a new urgency. I needed to go to Ellen—to put to rest the fears of the night. There was a light layer of fresh snow from last night's storm. I drove with caution, but inside I was racing again. Trying to get there. To keep something from happening. Tire marks in the driveway told me someone had either come or gone already. The house was quiet. No response to the door chimes. The shades were tightly drawn in the upstairs bedrooms. Ellen hadn't mentioned she was going away today.

By four that afternoon, when Ellen's phone still went unanswered, my worst fears took over. I remembered the despondency in her voice, the vacancy in her eyes. "What's left to live for?" she had said to me on our first trip downtown to the lawyer's office. *Oh, Lord. How could I have been so naïve? Please don't let her do anything desperate.*

My survival instinct took over. I dialed Mark at his office. Almost before I hung up the phone he was on his way home. I tried her number one more time. We would go over and break into her house if necessary. I heard the click and held my breath. Ellen's voice was weak and sounded far away.

"I had to get away by myself, Ruth, so I took the kids to a sitter and drove over by the lake for the day." I saw Ellen on snow-covered roads, following an ice-jammed lakeshore, going nowhere. Wandering idly through a cold, gray January day in territory she didn't even know.

"Ellen," I said firmly. I felt my strength returning. "Ellen, you must get some help. I can't help you any more. You need someone who knows what to do for you. Someone trained. I'm coming over. I'll bring some phone numbers. We're going to talk about it, and then you're going to call one of the numbers. Tonight." I hardly recognized my own voice. Ellen didn't object; but she usually didn't object to my suggestions. She just seemed relieved to have me tell her what to do.

I felt like I'd just crawled out from under the boulder. Now it was resting on someone else's shoulders—shoulders I knew wouldn't be crushed by its weight—professional shoulders that could help without absorbing. I was beginning to see the difference. That night I slept without interruption—for the first time in many, many nights.

Three weeks later I watched the DC-10 lift off into the winds toward the northwest. Ellen and the four children were aboard. "I've got to go home to mother's for a while," Ellen told me one day shortly after her first appointment with a counselor. "I just need time to put it all back together. I promise I'll get help out there." Her hands were still shaking and her coat button was still missing.

"I think that would be good, Ellen. Real good."

Now I watched as the powerful jets boosted the giant aircraft into its ascent. I didn't know when I'd see Ellen again. I'd helped her pack. Her house was for sale. She was gone. But I was left with a dried-up reservoir. I wasn't sure I had any personal resources left to give.

"Lord, I'm so tired. So empty." I allowed the tears to flow freely as I drove home from the airport. Relieving tears. Lubricating tears. Restoring tears. "Lord, please don't ask me to be a friend again. Not for a long, long time. I can't go through it again."

Over the days that followed, I boarded up the willing fragments of my servanthood and began my withdrawal. Servicing a friend costs too much. It draws the blood from your veins, saps strength from your days. You give and you're asked for more. You walk a mile and the signs say "two." You set the injured on your own horse and cancel your personal business to care for another's wounds. And when it's all over, you're left holding the bill.

You pay. You pay dearly. Sometimes, in the aftermath, resentment builds. Used. Disposed. Like a crumpled paper cup that no longer holds water. You write "Going Out of Business" across the Good Samaritan that is in you, and you keep yourself on the far side—the safe side—of the Jericho road.

In fact, you keep yourself from another friendship because friendship inevitably involves crisis. A friend sticks around when the pressure is on. And since a friend's pressure becomes your pressure, you avoid the risk. You become aloof and remote to keep from feeling another's pain.

Until, with the turn of the seasons, frozen streams are thawed and you learn to give again.

PART II

Celebration of Spring

⁘ 7 ⁘

Refill the Streams

Spring this year brought refreshing rains. They refilled the nearly empty reservoirs, reactivated the dormant chlorophyll, triggered growth, and revived the farmers' hopes for a fruitful year. The water table, however, did not replenish itself overnight. The long, dry months of seasons past had disrupted nature's delicate balance. Not to the extent of an actual drought, but to the extent that the parched earth was not producing at maximum efficiency. Revitalization would take time and plenty of persistent showers.

And the showers came cascading from the heavens and inundating the earth. I felt their force as they bombarded my car so fast that the wipers, even on top speed, could not keep the windshield clear.

I parked and walked the rest of the way to the lecture hall in the rain. It was only two more blocks, and the showers had a soothing effect on me. They were like the rejuvenation taking place slowly, silently, and almost unconsciously within me. Tiny rivulets of freshness rolled down my umbrella, spattered against the sidewalk, and soaked my legs and feet on the rebound. I felt the urge to kick off my shoes, fold my umbrella, and celebrate the rain like I had as a child, letting its coolness run onto my skin.

But propriety restrained me. Maturity overruled. I kept my umbrella properly over my head and meticulously avoided even the periphery of the puddles—for the sake of the people to whom I would be speaking in twenty minutes.

Strangers, most of them. Writers and would-be-writers. One-timers in my life. No need for personal involvement. Simply deliver my lecture notes with ease, humor, and professional expertise. Polite formalities. Detached interaction. Simple assignment. One I was used to performing. Surround yourself with many people and you don't feel obligated to give anyone the key to come inside. Hold them at a distance and they won't cost you anything. Keep them outside and you won't get hurt. I was good at self-defense.

After the lecture we stood around the front of the auditorium in a semicircle and talked specifics: what to do with this piece of poetry, where to send a true adventure, how to build suspense into a fictional short story. Being confident enough in my craft to help others felt good. I could help them and then go home. No one would wake me up in the middle of the night and ask me how to write a lead sentence or paragraph.

"Could I save you a seat for the banquet tonight?" The petite brunette before me hadn't waited to ask me a question about writing, only if I'd join her for dinner. My immediate impression was that she could probably answer some of my questions about writing. Her poise and confidence gave me the hint. We planned our five o'clock connection and she moved on. I noted how classy her off-white, two-piece suit looked and how straight her back was when she walked. *A pleasant option for a dinner partner*, I thought as she moved away. I hadn't planned on it being anything more than that.

"Tell me about yourself," Audra said as we finished our tomato juice and worked our way through sesame rolls and spinach salad. She leaned forward and waited for my response like she'd forgotten everyone else in the room. Her ability to concentrate on one person, especially in the middle of so many distractions, amazed me.

I stopped and thought about her question. I didn't remember having been asked it before, at least not in that exact way. Not "tell me about your writing, your speaking, your children, your husband," but "tell me about you." I wasn't sure I knew what to do with her question.

"I'm working on a book project right now in connection with my master's degree. I have several classes to finish up yet in between caring for a four-year-old and an eight-year-old. Our family camps now and then. Mark is a pastor. What about you?"

I had the feeling I hadn't really answered her question. She didn't know much more about me after hearing my answer than she did after reading the brochure blurb that listed conference personnel. My response was the kind I was used to giving, even to non-strangers. Audra got the standard rerun.

When Audra began talking about her publishing successes, something stirred inside me. She wasn't flaunting them; after all, I'd asked her. She was working on numerous magazine articles, some small book projects with a religious publishing house, and had negotiations under way with another. Her background was English literature—a master's degree plus—and several years of teaching on the college level. Teaching college was one of my secret ambitions, but I'd never been offered a job. I found my thoughts directing themselves inward—a turn I didn't enjoy but which sometimes happened anyway. *What am I doing leading this seminar? Audra is the college professor.*

By the time the waitresses had cleared away our dessert plates and we had turned our chairs to face the speaker, I'd noticed many other contrasts between Audra and me.

Her husband, Bill, was in the top management levels of a large chemical company headquartered in the south. She bore the stamp of southern aristocracy. Gracious. Poised. Refined. Gentle speech and movement. Even the way she dressed told me she knew what was proper and fitting; that she knew how to create beauty out of the ordinary.

She and her family had just moved into the area from a southern California beach town. I was certain I still saw traces of a California sun tan, even though they'd been in the Midwest for several months. Audra could talk with ease about almost any part of the country. She'd been almost everywhere. A cosmopolitan woman. The label, I decided was appropriate for Audra. She was out of my class—someone to admire from a distance. She appeared to have the good fortune that, in my discontented moments, I wished I could simply taste.

There was still a light drizzle at ten o'clock when I started for home. My headlights barely cut into the fog so I drove slowly, even though I knew the route well. FM 97—classical music for Chicago. I shifted mental gears from "The Role of Christian Journalism" to the Royal Philharmonic Orchestra and Rossini's *William Tell* Overture. I'd taught myself to leave my performances behind—to switch channels immediately and totally. A replay of how I did usually took as much energy as the real event. I didn't need the additional drain after an hour spent in front of an audience. I usually closed off the people and events surrounding the evening as well. However, the personalities of this particular evening were not easily forgotten—at least one of the personalities was not. . . .

It was early November and early morning when I saw Audra again. I spotted her as she and Bill came through the wide front doors of our church after the morning worship service. She waved in my direction, and we made our way toward each other through the crowd. Suddenly I felt like I'd known Audra for a long, long time. My greeting was enthusiastic.

"We may have found home today." Audra's voice and her smile were as bright and cheerful as the sparkling fall day. "We've been looking for a church ever since we moved to town." She turned toward Bill and introduced us. I sensed his genuineness and his warmth.

That same warmth drew me toward Bill and Audra the following Saturday at a church party. Almost automatically I found myself moving in their direction. At least my face would be one they'd recognize. I knew they were in a room full of strangers. My usual custom at church functions was to seek out strangers and introduce them to the old-timers.

But strangers didn't seem to be any major obstacle for Bill and Audra. By the time Mark and I reached them, they had met a couple we didn't know and introduced them to us.

"We felt we needed to get out and meet some people," Audra

volunteered. "This seemed like a good place to start."

We chatted for a while, and then Mark and I moved on to the hors d'oeuvres at the other end of the room. I felt a little disappointed as we walked away. Usually there was something I could do for newcomers, but Bill and Audra were fitting in quite well on their own. Sometimes self-sufficient people made me uneasy—I didn't know where to plug in with them. Usually it didn't bother me very long; but for some reason, it was different with Audra.

I was even more uneasy after Mark and I were invited to their home for dinner several weeks later. When Audra gave me their address, I knew we would be dining in one of the more picturesque neighborhoods of our town. Wide, winding streets. Immaculate landscapes. Sprawling designs of timber, stone, and brick— monuments to a builder's craft and an owner's money.

As soon as we got inside the door, however, Bill and Audra made all my uneasiness disappear. But I did find myself making comparisons. I sat down on the stone hearth in the rustic family room, basked in its warmth, and admired its authenticity. "I miss a fireplace—grew up with one that was our primary source of heat. On nights when Gulf breezes turned icy, we'd sleep in front of the fire. I guess that's why I mind so much not having one now."

Audra's house was filled with things she'd created herself. I asked about the needlepoint bellpull that hung in the front hall and the twin pine-cone wreaths that decorated the double doors. She'd made them both. I had a needlepoint chair cover that I'd started seven years before and a pine-cone wreath too, but I'd bought mine in the mountains of North Carolina from one of the local mountain craft shops. I laughed as I told Audra, but I resolved to work on my needlepoint the next day.

We wandered through the rusts, blues, and off-whites of the spacious two-story colonial house. The colors blended together into a tasteful, restful whole, reminding me of the walls at home that needed to be painted, the wallpaper and drapes that needed to be coordinated, and the checkerboard effect of multi-colored carpet that needed to be replaced—all waiting for a loosening of the cash flow that would come someday. Someday in the future.

Must remember to call some jeweler about the corrosion spots on my silver, I thought to myself as I picked up a sparkling, sterling fork. I noticed the spots on my silver-plated flatware every time I used it to entertain company. Audra's sterling reminded me, and I made a mental note.

The evening moved along with ease and comfort. I watched the candlelight play on the centerpiece—an arrangement of white button mums and short-needled pine set in a silver bowl—and half-listened as Bill and Mark discussed the future of the chemical industry in relationship to the possibilities of mining the ocean floors.

Then Audra turned the conversation in a more personal direction. She looked at me when she spoke. "You must feel some pressure now and then from your role as a pastor's wife. What kinds of unusual struggles are there for public people like you and Mark?"

I stopped my coffee cup in midair. How did she know I felt pressures? Was I looking pressured tonight? Were there dark circles under my eyes? Did my hands shake? I always tried to keep struggles well hidden. A pastor's wife can never reveal her pressure points, especially to members of the congregation. Pressure comes from not trusting God, and who would admit they were guilty of that? I wished I'd joined the discussion on mining minerals from the ocean floor. It would have been a safer conversation. But Audra had directed her question to me, and it was up to me to answer.

"Pressures? Oh, I'm sure every job has pressures connected with it, but the rewards of being a pastor's wife far outweigh the negatives—I meet lots of interesting people, get to travel some with Mark, plus there's the satisfaction gained from helping people. I probably don't feel many more pressures than you do as the wife of a regional manager for Allied Chemicals."

Again, it was the kind of answer I was used to giving. And again I had the feeling that I hadn't answered Audra's question. I was not used to her kind of questions. It would be some time before I would understand them or be willing to answer them. To do that meant letting people inside. I wasn't sure I was ready for that yet. But having someone ask me those kinds of questions gave me a warm feeling—like the glow from the candlelight on the dining room table had moved inside me. Audra seemed to be a person who would wait for an answer. What's more, I found myself hoping she would, but hardly daring to believe it.

The next morning I called a jeweler to find out what to do about corroding silver-plate and got out the needlepoint I hadn't worked on for at least nine months. I determined that I would do at least two rows of needlepoint a day, accompanied by a cup of my favorite coffee blend to make the task more tolerable. There was no reason why I could not have homemade touches to decorate my house, too.

Winter's snow was turning to slush when Audra called one morning about three weeks later. Slush is hard to forget, especially when it has just been deposited at six-inch intervals right through the middle of your brown-and-gold braided rug. For the second time that morning my four-year-old had forgotten to remove his boots when he came in the door. The phone rang while I was still trying to scrape the frozen grime from between the ridges of braid and supervise the picking up of a trail of soaked mittens, scarf, snow pants, hat, and jacket. The rest of my morning's emotional resources had been spent recovering from a mess left by a leaky sink faucet and from discovering a computer error in our checking account. An early-morning call from the bank had informed me that our account was overdrawn by $289.73 and that our checks were being returned.

"Tell me about things at the Senter's house." The soft southern drawl at the other end of the line made my early-morning series of catastrophies seem like a bad dream. *Things can't possibly be this gloomy. I must not have gotten enough sleep last night. Pull yourself together, Ruth. Your nerves should not be this thin.*

"Well, would you believe the snow's melting. The icicles have been dripping all morning. Jori has a half-day of school today and tomorrow—teacher's institute. Mark is gone for three days— soaking up the sun in Nashville. How nice of you to call."

"How do you react to that—Mark running off to the sunbelt and leaving you with two days of teacher's institute and drippy icicles besides?" She gave me hints that she'd been there.

"Oh, we have our ups and downs, but we'll make it. A lot of wives have it worse than I do. Mark travels so seldom in comparison, I really have no room to complain. Have you all licked the flu? When is your trip south? How did your neighborhood potluck go? Did you find a dentist?"

Keep her talking. Cover up with questions. Turn the tables. That way you don't have to talk about yourself and run the risk of leaking information that would jeopardize your strong-woman image. For the third time I'd given Audra my standard response to personal questions. Pretend you don't have black slush meshed into your rug, the sink faucet isn't leaking, and your checks aren't bouncing.

Audra started to wind things up. "Well, I won't keep you. I didn't call for any particular reason. I guess I just needed to hear a cheerful voice. February days in Illinois are hard on my spirits. I felt about as gray as the clouds this morning. I miss California on days like today." She seemed to be having second thoughts about hanging up.

"I've been worried about Josh, too. His teacher feels he's not responding as well as they had hoped he would. He goes in for more tests tomorrow. Some days I think that finding out your child has learning disabilities is like looking up at a thousand-foot cliff and knowing you have to climb it, but feeling like you don't have the strength and know-how to even start. Some days it hits me harder than others—like today."

I felt my spirit returning. "I'm so glad you felt free to call, Audra. Please do it anytime. It must be difficult. I'll be praying about Josh's tests tomorrow. What time are they? As for today, doesn't a good book in front of the fire sound good? Why don't you try it? You might even forget the slush outside. We do have spring in Illinois, remember? Just think how much you will enjoy summer after you've been through this."

I gave her my cheerful pep talk and then hung up the phone. The slush in my rug, the leaks under my sink, and the tangled finances at the bank hadn't gone away. Glancing at the clock, I realized I had fifteen minutes to get to the bank to sign some papers before the accountant left for the day. Nicky's snowsuit was dripping wet. So were his boots. Jori would be home in half an hour for lunch and the breakfast dishes were still stacked in my leaky sink. I was afraid to run any water. I sat down at the kitchen table and rested my pounding head against my arms. The muscles in my shoulders felt like taut rubber bands.

"Oh, Lord. A few minor irritations like this should not be destroying me. There must be something good about this day. Show me, please." I cried even though I'd just prayed. Nicky brought me a Kleenex to wipe my tears. He stood beside me and watched while I blew my nose. His blue eyes were large and concerned. I stood up abruptly, resolved to conquer the mountain. It was silly to cry. I'd make it. I always did.

The slush did turn to spring. The world popped out of its winter hibernation again and the daylight hours lengthened. I was convinced that Audra was someone I enjoyed being with. At times I thought she was like a wide-open door—inviting and hospitable, welcoming me into her home and into her life. She offered me the pieces of her background, slowly and sensitively, as though she was constructing a mosaic of her life so I could understand the total picture. Sometimes the pieces were surprisingly tragic, but she offered those segments of her life to me with as much candor and grace as she did the usual, happy ones.

We'd just finished an Easter vacation lunch on her back porch. The children were off in the woods that provided treehouses, rope swings, and backyard fun and adventure. Audra had served us barbecue on white china plates accented with a bright yellow lemon and mint green tea leaves design. The straw placemats were yellow and shaped like lemons. We used green napkins and drank a frosty mint punch with slices of lemon floating on the surface. The day was unusually warm for April.

Audra brought up the subject; I never had to ask. "I haven't told you much about my mother. She was an alcoholic. Finally things got so bad she had to be institutionalized. Daddy was always busy supervising the textile mills." She did not pause. Apparently, this was a story Audra was ready to tell. "It got kind of lonely rattling around in a big old house with no brothers or sisters. Before she was hospitalized mother was either gone to one of her clubs or sleeping off the good time from the day before. The shades in her room were often drawn, and her head usually hurt so bad that she couldn't even stand to have me sit on the edge of her bed." Audra's voice was wistful. She took a sip of her lemonade, then tucked her legs up underneath her on the chaise lounge. "I never will forget all the Christmases I was driven to my aunties because mother was so drunk she couldn't get out of bed. Mother died on Christmas day. She didn't even know who I was when I called to say Merry Christmas."

Audra's voice faded, and her eyes seemed to look into the far away and long ago. Neither of us spoke for a while. I leaned my chin in my hands and stared out at the leafy woods. It was hard for me to put together the Audra who sat before me and the child Audra who had everything except a mother.

I was moved by her story—not to pity, but to a far greater respect. I didn't feel compelled to say anything or to quote Romans 8:28 and remind her that all things work together for good to those who love God. What's more, I didn't feel I needed to do anything for her; so I said simply, "Thanks for sharing that part of yourself with me. I never would have guessed."

It didn't occur to me until I was driving home how difficult it might have been for her to tell me her story. I'd seen pain in her eyes. Her father had died within two years of her mother. She knew what it was to be alone. My struggles seemed miniscule in comparison.

"We really should have Bill and Audra over sometime," I said to Mark one night during the summer as we drove home from their house. We'd seen a movie together and had topped it off with French silk pie in their breakfast nook. Actually, I'd thought of inviting them several times, but there was always one more project I wanted to get done first. It was a convenient time to talk to Mark about projects.

"Let's finish stripping the bedroom chest, refinish it, get the bathroom wallpaper up, and then do some entertaining. I've lost track of the times we've been to Bill and Audra's, and they have yet to come here."

I was beginning to feel a little guilty. It was so easy to accept Audra's gracious hospitality. I knew she loved entertaining. And for her it came so easy. One of these days I'd get around to inviting company. But I had to get ready first, especially since the company was used to designer prints, original oils, and perfectly matched color schemes. For some reason I thought those things mattered to Bill and Audra. It took a summer afternoon and a trip into the city to show me differently.

"Ever tasted Godiva chocolate? My very favorite. It's manufactured in Belgium, and packed in Connecticut. Here, let me treat you to a taste?" Audra stopped by the display of gold boxes trimmed with pink velvet roses and ribbon. The rich, creamy flavor awakened every taste bud in my mouth and left its fresh aftertaste lingering for the rest of the morning. "Godiva and Ghirardelli are some of the world's finest chocolates, I've decided." Audra apparently knew one chocolate from another.

We moved on through the colonnade of white marble and sprawling green ferns that were fed sunlight through a transparent dome far overhead. The rotunda ceiling was pieced together with exquisite patterns of Byzantine tiles. Audra continued the chocolate theme as we walked. "Ghirardelli is made in San Francisco. The factory's been there since just after the Gold Rush. It's worth the trip to San Francisco just to visit Ghirardelli Square and the chocolate factory. Did you know that Columbus discovered cacao beans in a canoe he intercepted off the Mexican coast on his fourth voyage to the New World? Took the beans back to Queen Isabella and chocolati soon became the official drink of her royal court. Just thought you might need to know that for the next article you write."

She laughed, and we turned our conversation to lunchtime in the English Room. We worked our way up seven flights of escalators. Each level afforded a panoramic view of the vast array of costly merchandise collected from all corners of the world and brilliantly displayed in one of Chicago's more prestigious centers of commerce.

We waited at the corner of a red and black tartan carpeted room. The high beamed ceilings and the trestle tables with their tall, straight-backed wooden benches reminded me of one of Oxford University's great halls. The memory brought with it a shadow of hurt. We could see beyond the variegated rooftops out to the lake where white sailboats capped the blue. It was a picturesque scene once you got over the three blocks of steel and concrete. We asked for a seat beside a window.

The food didn't really remind me of England; but that was all right; the atmosphere did. We were there for each other and not for the food anyhow. Conversation was light until Audra sat down her blue and white Spode coffee cup with deliberateness and took a deep breath.

"You know, I met Ruth Senter over a year ago and there are still big chunks of you I don't know—gaping holes. I can't piece you all together. You haven't provided me with enough background to do it. Sometimes that's terribly frustrating to me.

"Take your house for example. Do you know, I've never even seen where you live?" (I knew it very well, but I didn't say so.) "It's like you're a verse out of context. I can't visualize your surroundings—how you look when you're settled down for the evening in your family room, or how you operate when you're fixing dinner in your kitchen.

"To be perfectly honest with you, I was hurt the other day when you told me you were having the Thompsons and the Bowens over because they were new in the church and hadn't gotten to meet many people yet. I never got that kind of invitation from you, and I consider us good friends."

She paused, took a sip of her coffee, and dabbed her lips lightly with her napkin. She looked relieved that she'd said it. "I just felt I needed to let you know what's inside me. I like you, Ruth. I care about you a great deal. And I'd like to get to know the real Ruth inside, if you'll let me. But I won't force myself. I guess I have too much pride for that. I'm not asking that you respond, only that you understand I'm feeling held at a distance—and that hurts."

Far away, over the rooftops, the little white sailboats skirted the waves. Vague. Indefinable. Picturesque and pretty from a distance. But sailboats weren't built to create a pretty picture. They were built to be experienced. I saw myself in those sailboats. Vague. Indefinable. Skirting the waves. Someone had just asked to come on board. I had no idea yet how I would respond. I'd been used to distance for a long, long time, and I wasn't sure yet that I could risk the change.

Open Doors

"Is *this* where you live?" Jori's little friend prolonged the "this" for emphasis. I couldn't tell whether she was registering awe or disappointment as I pushed the garage door opener and pulled the Vega into its half of the two-car garage. The other side was the only playroom our house could hold—an oddly arranged playhouse, partitioned off with old trunks, steel files, and folding chairs; a "Matchbox" race track weaved in and out along the cement floor, and old green and brown washbaskets held outdoor and garage-type toys. "Nice house," she added almost as an afterthought as I helped her from the back seat.

I agreed. It was a nice house. Cozy and warm. The first we'd ever owned. My brother Ed had painted it during his spring break from college. Light green. Not because I especially liked green, but because that's the color of the paint that was left by the former owners. I could live with green. There were a lot of things about the house I'd learned to live with. Usually it didn't matter too much. A home is for loving, for learning, for growing. Who cares that the carpets are red, green, blue, and two different shades of gold? Who cares that some of the brown tiles in the family room are cracked and need replacing but have to remain because the former owners used up all the brown tiles and you can't afford new ones?

When you're reading bedtime stories and giving good-night kisses, you don't think of the fact that Jori is sleeping on a bedframe that you salvaged out of the neighbor's garbage. You don't think of the fact that her dresser, that you painted yellow and lime green was one that your friend's eighty-year-old grandmother was going to give to a rescue mission before you rescued it. A home is for hugging and kissing and touching.

So the pink and green bathroom may not go with anything else in the house; and the sterile, formal, all-in-a-row arrangement of blue junipers, yews, and yucca plants set in white stone may not fit your natural, back-to-the-woods landscaping tastes; but this was home. The place where children sometimes rang the doorbell so hard they pushed the button back into a hole nobody can reach into; and where someone accidentally swung a bat too close to the house and left a distinct bat impression right next to the garage door; and where children once leaned against the front hallway and left greasy handprints all over the pale blue and white striped wallpaper which had just been hung.

A home is a background for enjoying people, not for showing off one's skills at interior decorating. It reflects love, not money; care for one another, not how clever you are with light, color, and texture.

I knew the intangible meanings of home. I had carefully thought through what values mattered most in our family and in our home. I knew that kindness, warmth, and love make a house a home, not colors, designs, and furniture. And yet tonight, when I saw the headlights in the driveway and heard the doorbell ring, my perspective on home suddenly bounced out of focus again.

I welcomed Bill into the living room but hurriedly called to Mark, grabbed my coat from the closet, and rushed us all out the door and on our way to the annual church dinner. Bill and Audra had planned to pick us up since the restaurant was at our end of town.

"Wish we didn't have to hurry. I'd have invited you in." I offered my excuse as I slid into the back seat. As soon as I said it, I knew I didn't really mean it. I was relieved that we were running a little late. Audra might have recognized my excuse, but she graciously said, "Maybe next time." Next time I would do it. Late or not. I made my resolution with a certain skepticism. I'd let myself down this time.

Earlier that afternoon as I vacuumed and dusted, performing my normal, dispassionate, Saturday ordeal, I had planned on inviting Audra and Bill in. It was time I showed them where we lived, even if it was just a quick little tour. After my downtown lunch last month with Audra, I realized the significance of an invitation to our house. Audra had been honest enough to tell me it mattered to her. The ball was in my court now. I knew it. But somehow, at the last minute, I changed my mind. I hadn't yet gotten all my projects done. Our bedroom dresser was still nursery red and white and the bathroom wallpaper was still a pink-green combination that was coming off the walls at the seams.

The more I knew of Audra, the more certain I became that my home decor didn't matter to her. But I had yet to convince my heart. It still mattered to me. Her friendship was too important. I had to be sure. I had to prove to her that I was the competent wife, mother, friend, cook, homemaker, interior designer, professional I wanted to be.

Home is where people love each other. But it is also where you are the most vulnerable. Sometimes, in the beginning, the more a person means to you, the harder it is to be vulnerable—to welcome them into a high-risk place. You want so much to succeed with them. And so you leak information a little at a time—safe information. When you're not sure, you build a dam to hold back the flow. There comes a time, however, when you unlock the flood gates, even though you may not think you are ready. Then it is too late to stop the current. You are known. . . .

"Jori, please close the front door," I yelled through the house. "You're letting in the cold." The day was chilly even for early October, and there was no reason to try to prolong summer by keeping the doors open.

"But, mother," came back the persistent wail, "I can't close the door. They're here."

I gazed around the room in panic. Breakfast dishes to finish. A basket of towels and washcloths yet to fold. And beds to make. They'd been stripped to put on fresh sheets for grandma and grandpa, who were due in from Pennsylvania on the 4:30 train that afternoon. We'd planned a day at the apple orchards until then. And now Bill, Audra, and the boys were sitting in the driveway waiting for us. According to my meticulously planned schedule for our early-morning, pre-apple-orchard routine, we should have finished everything ten minutes ago. Everyone had been given a chore. But somewhere the system had broken down, and I was flying around in animated suspension, wondering what to do next.

"Invite them in." Mark's voice came from the kitchen where he was finishing the dishes.

"Yes, do invite them in," I said as I rushed to the door to welcome them. My hiding game was over.

I felt the crisp fall day just beyond the open door, like a new dollar bill that had never been folded. The rustle of leaves. The smell of apples and spices and pumpkins in the air. Autumn. Friends coming up your front walk. Good friends. People you love and care for. Audra in a bright red V-neck sweater, white blouse, and blue jeans; Bill with his plaid flannel lumberman's shirt. Coffee still hot in the pot from breakfast. What a waste to worry about mismatched furniture, kaleidoscope carpet, and unmade beds. What a sin to be so concerned about your house that you can't relax and enjoy people, to assume that friends won't accept you because your wallpaper is the wrong color.

I opened wide the front door and gave everybody hugs as they stepped inside. "Come in. Come in." And this time I really meant it. I felt myself unwinding inside. "Let's sit down and have a cup of coffee. Then we'll put you to work. With a doubled workforce we can be ready in fifteen minutes."

And we were. After our coffee, I showed Audra where the company sheets were kept, directed Bill to a dishtowel, sent the children to the back-yard swing, breathed a sigh of relief, and set about to fold the still-warm-from-the-dryer towels and washcloths. About midway through the basket I remembered that Adura would see the tattered, white-turned-yellow mattress cover that I'd been meaning to replace for the last two years. It covered a hand-me-down mattress from Mark's folks. *Oh, well.* I surprised myself with my complacency. Strangely enough, I didn't even feel a need to go into the bedroom and explain to her about the mattress cover that I'd never gotten around to replacing. Suddenly, I was just glad she was there sharing my house with me—my simple, three-bedroom ranch that Uncle Ed had painted green.

"Your house is just like you," Audra said as she came out of the bedroom with a pile of dirty sheets and pillowcases in her arms. "Warm and interesting. I love the arrangement of old pictures above your bed, and tell me about that antique secretary. I'm fascinated by its lines."

I gave her an abbreviated history of the desk, piled the sheets and pillowcases in the washer, grabbed the bushel baskets from the garage, and we were out the door and off to the orchards.

"Thanks for inviting us in," Audra said as we walked to the car. I knew what she was saying.

She'd understood my struggle all along. She seemed to know how hard it was for me not to compare, not to feel second-class. She was sensitive to how closely my ego was tied to my house. Some of it I'd told her. Some she'd picked up on her own. Today she saw my house with all its undone projects, and yet I felt myself relaxing in the security of her friendship.

"I'm not looking for a perfect friend, or a friend's perfect house," she'd said that day while we watched little white sailboats from the seventh-story restaurant. "I wouldn't feel at home." Today I believed that she really meant what she'd said. She'd given me permission to be myself. I had yet to learn to do the same for her. . . .

"How about coming over for a piece of pie. I'd serve you homemade, but all my homemade pies are in the freezer waiting for out-of-town company; so we'll have to settle for Poppin' Fresh. I will brew you some fresh coffee, though."

I extended my humorous invitation to Bill and Audra one night after church. At least I thought I was being humorous. Both Audra and Bill knew I was not Betty Crocker or the Pillsbury Dough Boy when it came to the culinary arts. They knew there were no homemade pies in my freezer. I figured laughing about it would relieve some of the pressure.

Audra laughed, but down deep I wasn't sure she was enjoying my wit. She must have recognized that my attempt at humor was related to an afternoon earlier that week when I'd dropped by to deliver a book to her.

Audra's boys were out playing when I drove up. Bill was out of town on business. That day Audra's kitchen smelled like the Sara Lee test kitchens I'd often driven past on my way through one of our northern suburbs. Her kitchen looked like a Sara Lee kitchen, too. Cinnamon swirls. Nut and raisin bread. A Boston cream pie. Plus sparkling Mason quart jars filled with sweet applesauce and packaged with Audra's own sticker that said, "From Audra's Kitchen." It looked to me like she had enough applesauce to last through two winters. She was putting it on the shelves next to her homemade jellies and pickles. Her shelves reminded me of the farmers' markets we had back home in Lancaster, Pennsylvania. Nothing store-bought or artificially preserved in the entire market. Straight from the farmers' fields, the cook's kitchen.

"Bill's out of town and you're going to all this trouble to make these goodies?" I couldn't imagine it.

"When you enjoy cooking as much as I do, it's no trouble. Besides, Bill's folks will be here in another three weeks. I'll stick most of this in the freezer and not have to bother cooking while they're here. Have a cinnamon swirl. It's far enough away from dinner time."

She slid one of the still-steaming swirls onto an off-white ironstone dessert plate that was trimmed with a yellow and orange band. The plate trim perfectly matched the accent colors in her kitchen wallpaper.

"You are truly amazing, Audra. Here you are with your meals prepared a month in advance. I have trouble keeping up with each day. Taking pies out of boxes takes a lot of time and energy, you know."

I meant to give Audra a compliment. I wanted her to know how much I respected her abilities at creative homemaking. I had yet to realize that my backhanded compliments always contained comparisons. Evidently, I was still not comfortable with one or the other of us.

It showed up again tonight as I cut into the Poppin' Fresh lemon meringue pie. I felt I had to explain. "Poppin' Fresh sure comes in handy after a busy weekend. I spent all of yesterday on a seminar at church. Friday night at the ladies' group fall kick-off. It doesn't leave much time for home-cooking. This weekend we've kind of eaten on the run. Can't imagine you ever serving pie from a box."

"I do sometimes." Audra's voice was matter-of-fact. "Please don't apologize, Ruth. Poppin' Fresh is a special treat. Bill doesn't buy it for me very often. Says it's too expensive a habit, and I love it."

The next week when I saw Audra at church, she handed me a little package of recipe cards tied together with yellow yarn. The attached note said, "Some quick, easy recipes for my friend who cooks and eats on the run. P.S. Thanks for sharing your lemon meringue pie. It was delicious. I don't care who made it."

The apple harvest ended. Autumn foliage gave up the fight against winter winds, and thoughts turned toward the holidays. Christmas—a time for the gourmet cooks to shine and the writers who are also would-be cooks to panic.

Somewhere between writing deadlines, Christmas shopping, banquet devotionals, Sunday school practices and programs, holiday choir concerts, staff parties, school parties, church parties, and neighborhood parties, my domestic endeavors got squeezed in. I rushed through three dozen each of our traditional holiday spritz, sand tarts, and sugared nut drops. Tied up in a wooden strawberry box with a red and green plaid ribbon, they made attractive little gifts for Jori and Nicky to deliver to the neighbors.

The children complained that our supply was too low—that we gave them all away and never had enough left to eat for ourselves. The thought that tomorrow I'd whip up another batch usually proved to be just that—a thought. Baking cookies was no small undertaking, especially with seven different kinds of decorations to mix and match, two eager but untrained assistants, and one supervisor who felt the need to do ten different things at once and seemed to have only thumbs with which to do them. Christmas baking was not my idea of fun and relaxation; it was something that had to be done.

Things were different for Audra. Much different. Her invitation came in a green envelope, written on a green and gold card:

HOLIDAY BUFFET
SATURDAY, DECEMBER 18TH
6:30 P.M.
BILL'S AND AUDRA'S

I knew immediately that it would not be a paper-plate, potluck affair. Audra would shine on this one, along with her sterling and crystal and gold-rimmed Lenox china. I was fully prepared to savor and enjoy, but I did feel somewhat obligated to at least offer my assistance, especially when I learned she'd invited fifteen couples.

"I don't want you to do a thing except just come and enjoy the evening," Audra answered when I volunteered to bring a dessert or two. "Bill is a terrific assistant when it comes to things like this, and besides, I already have half of it done and in the freezer."

I laughed. "I could have predicted that you would. I'm still amazed at how you do it all."

Audra smiled. "Don't try to figure it out. We're different. Let's just enjoy each other's differences. I love every minute of entertaining thirty people, but I have yet to understand how you can write an entire book in nine months. I guess we're even."

The evening was everything I predicted it would be and even more. Candles, supported in sand-filled bags, lined the driveway. A giant garland of fresh greens, highlighted with red velvet, outlined the front double doors. Inside, there was a holiday blend of balsam and pine, nutmeg and cinnamon stick, apple cider and lemon, and spicy aromas drifting from the wassail bowl.

Audra sparkled. So did her two-story colonial—clear, miniature lights nestled among the boughs of the ten-foot Douglas fir that stood in one corner of the family room; a refracted rainbow bounced off the crystal evergreen that presided over the butler's table in the living room; a fire blazed on the hearth; and candles beamed from the window ledges.

The dining room table was a smorgasbord of wonder and delight—an artistic design of edible cornucopias, fold-ups, pinwheels, trees, stars, and balls, shrimp wheels, ham and cheese puffs, smoked salmon rolls, stuffed mushrooms, avocado-beef spread, hot cheese-chive dip, pâté with crackers, mint punch, chewy nut bars, red and green sugar cookies of all shapes and sizes, tiny mocha cream puffs, fruit cake. The array brought sighs of approval and admiration. Audra's table was truly a work of art.

As I passed through the line, I stuck my head into the kitchen where Audra was refilling the punch bowl. "What a spread, Audra. It's beautiful. You've done it again, only this time you really outdid yourself." Audra looked uncomfortable with my praise. I thought it a bit strange. Compliments did not usually seem hard for her to handle. She smiled and said simply, "Thank you, Ruth. Please enjoy it."

I turned to Audra's neighbor who was behind me in line. "And I'm lucky to get a few dozen cookies made by Christmas Eve. Isn't this amazing?" We both agreed that when it came to cooking and entertaining, Audra knew how to do it.

I pointed out the centerpiece—red crocheted Christmas balls put together in the shape of a Christmas tree. Audra, I knew, had created every stitch of her centerpiece by hand.

"Makes me wonder what I do with my time," I added half-jokingly. If I had stopped to think about it, I would have realized that that's really what bothered me. It took someone else to bring it to my attention. . . .

February was a dull month that needed some life, and today was a drab day that needed some color. Somewhere in my card shop browsing, I'd come across a card that said, "A friend is someone with whom you dare to be yourself." It was perfect for Audra, so I bought it and waited for an occasion to give it. Today seemed to be the occasion.

I signed the card, "Thanks for your friendship." A deep purple hyacinth plant from the florist and a package of blueberry tea gave me reason for a quick, February drop-in celebration at Audra's house. I was on my way to the library near her end of town anyway.

I had research to do and Audra had a manuscript to type, so we'd planned on my visit being brief.

"I discovered this tea at a little spice and tea shop downtown. Smell it. I think it's meant for sharing. Not the kind you drink alone." I opened the bag and gave Audra a sniff as she filled her teapot with water, turned on the burner, and pulled a tray of Sara Lee blueberry muffins out of her freezer.

"Well, if that's the case, we'll just have to complement your tea with a treat from Sara Lee. Um, that tea smells good. So does the plant. I feel like June already. Thanks for turning my day into spring." She glanced at the hyacinth plant and popped the muffins into the oven.

"Sara Lee. In _your_ freezer?" My mind was quick to make the observation. "Well, welcome to the rank and file. That brings you down to the level of the rest of us. You _do_ cook from a box now and then." I'd meant it as a compliment—at least I thought I did. Audra felt beneath my words. She poured the tea and served the muffins with a suddenly methodical deliberateness—almost like our self-made spring had disappeared for a time. I recognized the symptoms in her movements.

"You've got something on your mind," was the only invitation she needed. I had the feeling she would have said it even without my invitation.

"May I tell you how your compliments come across to me? I get the feeling they're comparisons, that you're measuring us against each other. Sometimes I feel like you see me performing— showing off my home, my crafts, the food I create, the parties I give. It's almost like, around you, I'm not free to serve homemade cinnamon swirls or to create my own centerpiece or use my sterling. Those things are me, Ruth. I do them, not to prove I'm better than you or to put on a show for you, but because they are gifts from God that I find great pleasure in using to serve you and others.

"When you say things like, 'You do cook from a box, too,' that seems to me like a put-down—almost like I think of myself as too good to use Sara Lee or to eat Poppin' Fresh pies. Let me be me, Ruth. Let me enjoy serving you homemade cinnamon swirls and a nine-course dinner, if I want, without making me feel that I'm trying to outdo you or impress you. The greatest compliment you could give me is, 'I'm honored by the love you've shown me through this nine-course dinner or through this beautiful table you've set for me.' I invite you into my home, Ruth, to honor you, not to outdo you. Please understand. And please don't stop serving me Poppin' Fresh pies. It's the only time I get them.''

Then she laughed. And in her honesty I saw relief. Openness. Clarity. Transparency. Like words inked on a page for all to see. I knew what she was feeling. She'd left no doubt. Freedom to be herself was all she asked. No backhanded compliments. No yardsticks. No comparisons. No apologies for Poppin' Fresh pies or homemade cinnamon swirls.

As I drove toward the library through the monotony of February, I felt as though another layer of myself had been peeled away. Sometimes the exposure hurts, especially when it's from someone who matters to you. I'd always run from this kind of thing before because of the hurt. This time I had no desire to retreat, at least not for the present.

When Cold Winds Threaten

The Chicago River is the first river in the world made to flow away from its mouth. Billed as the "river that runs backwards," its waters were reversed during the late 1800s in a complicated showdown between nature and technology. The natural course of the river is eastward, through downtown Chicago, and into Lake Michigan. However, concerned because Chicago's pollution was being dumped into its lake, engineers turned the river in a westerly direction.

Today, giant metal locks hold Lake Michigan and the Chicago River at bay in the Chicago harbor. Instead of flowing into the lake, the south branch of the river now travels down the Chicago Ship and Sanitary Canal, joins the Des Plaines River further west, and eventually merges with the mother of all rivers, the Mississippi.

The average passerby would never know the Chicago River has done an about-face, unless of course, they knew the river before. Instead they are captured by the force, beauty, and versatility of its present course. In the winter, the river blows its icy breath onto foot commuters who cross any of its nineteen bridges or who scurry along toward the impressive array of steel, chrome, glass, marble, and terra cotta that house the riverfront in squares, rectangles, spheres, and triangles.

On March 17, green dye turns the river into an emerald salute to the large Irish ancestry at home within the city. In spring and summer, the waterway becomes a conveyor belt for pleasure craft, tugs, barges, and freighters from ports as far away as Sweden and Italy. The river opens it arms to native and foreigner alike—its "jackknife bridges" splitting in two, heaving their massive girders into the air, welcoming the river traffic into its channels.

Reversing the course of an entire river was no small accomplishment. It took a core of some eighty-five hundred skilled engineers and craftsmen almost seven years to complete the three-million-dollar project. But today, business continues as usual on the Chicago River. A few old-timers or history buffs can tell you how it used to be; but the rest of us take the river at face value, forgetting or overlooking the story of change that is a part of Chicago's blue-ribbon waterway.

Reversing the currents in one's personal life is not easy, either. Life change does not come without sacrifice and cost, whether it be reorienting values around God's standards or reprogramming responses to people. It is far easier and more comfortable to maintian the natural flow. Self-preservation. Self-sufficiency. Self-promotion. Self-discovery. Self-containment.

But every now and then, into a life come whisperings that old riverbeds, as deep and natural as they may seem, are not necessarily the best riverbeds. Sometimes the flow must change direction for the sake of the future. The current must be reversed or redirected. And when we're too close to ourselves to see the need, we must open our ears, our eyes, and our hearts to someone else. Sometimes we must depend on them to show us who we are and allow them to help change the flow.

So here we were—the river and I—companions in slow, tedious alterations. . . .

Today the river was a mirror—a watery image of the real thing. Audra and I could see ourselves duplicated in the blue-green—slight distortions, we depended on our knowledge of ourselves to bring about focus.

We were standing in the shadow of the Wrigley Building, looking out onto a wide, white liquid path that cut across almost the entire width of the river. It vaguely resembled the building's twenty-three stories of Gothic window casings, set one on top of the other, and topped off with a clock tower and a square crown. In its unmirrored form, the Wrigley Building looked almost like a giant vanilla birthday cake.

"Let's inspect the Marriott," Audra suggested as we caught our breath at the top of the stairs that led from the docks to Michigan Avenue. We faced north toward Chicago's "magnificent mile"—an array of costly shops, restaurants, and high-rise hotels that begin at the river and end at the lake.

"I've been wanting an excuse to get inside that hotel. We have forty-five minutes. Plenty of time," I agreed, and we turned to wave to our husbands who were waiting in the ticket line on the lower dock where our lakefront cruise was to originate.

The new Marriott hotel was spacious and grand enough to provide hours of pastime entertainment. We browsed the specialty shops in the lower lobby, scouted Allie's Bakery and the other restaurants on the fourth floor, checked out the ballroom on seventh, and relaxed in the Victorian velvet of the atrium lounge. We didn't talk about anything in particular—nothing serious or heavy. Just a time to enjoy. A filler in a schedule. An interlude in the day. Nothing boring or wasted about it. Typical of the times Audra and I spent together.

Fifteen minutes till cruise time, so we decided to head back toward the river, slowly and leisurely. No reason to hurry or worry, we thought. But when we got to the top of the winding cement stairs that led down to the dock, we saw the deckhands lifting the gangplank. The boat was filled, and somewhere on board were our husbands with our tickets. The captain blasted his final whistle into the otherwise peaceful afternoon. We bolted down the stairs, leaped onto the dock, and yelled to the skipper that we had tickets and were meant to be on board.

"Sorry, ladies. This boat is full." The rough and ready mate continued to loosen the ropes and lock up the gangplank. "Next boat leaves an hour and a half from now."

"But our husbands are on there. We have tickets for this cruise. There must be room." I felt the pressure mounting in my temples, and my voice screamed in competition against the roar of the engines. We had to get on that boat. Every ounce of my energy was flowing toward that end.

"These boat rides don't have reserved seating, ma'am. We don't wait for nobody. Now if you stand there you're going to get hit by flying ropes, and it won't be my fault. Not my fault you weren't here on time either. Stand back please." He seemed bent on keeping us from that ride. In the jumble I saw Mark coming from the other side of the boat, starting toward the raised gangplank.

"Sir, you have to let us on that boat. We have tickets." I felt like I was a siren.

"Oh, come on, Stu. Let the ladies on. It'll only take a second to lower the plank." A much more kindly deckhand pleaded our case. He obviously had some influence, for the gangplank was lowered.

As I followed Audra across, my knees shook. Stu scowled at me as I stepped over the coiled rope, and under his breath he spit his vulgar revenge directly into my face. I felt my whole body catch fire. I had just been reduced to scum. Furiously I followed Audra to the seats Bill and Mark were holding for us on the other side of the boat. The whistle repeated itself and the shore began to slip away.

Apparently Stu had no sooner gotten the gangplank back in place when he came around to continue his vengeance. I saw him coming and felt my stomach recoil. He hadn't said it all the first time. Only this time my whole insides stood up to him—before I even knew what I was doing. I was ready to strike back.

"Listen, mister, I don't have to take that from you. If I ruined your day, that's your problem. But I'm not about to let you ruin mine. Get off my case." There was fire in my words. In my eyes. In my chest. I felt my heart accelerating. Mark had risen from the row behind me and was about to lend his force when Stu apparently decided it would be in his best interest to move along.

I said I wasn't going to let him ruin my day, but I felt he already had. I felt angry. Insulted. Humiliated in front of a boat full of people.

"Hey, I'm glad to see you have some spunk in you. You do get angry." Audra attempted to relieve the pressure. She only made it worse. She'd spotted my anger. What's more, I had verbalized it. What kind of a Christian testimony was it to yell at the deckhand? Where was my patience? My love? My long-suffering? "Blessed are the peacemakers. . . ." I was beginning to feel I'd failed on all accounts. Most of all, Audra had seen the raw ingredients—the "me" under pressure. And I didn't like what I'd shown her.

"Sorry about that." I turned around to extend my apologies to Mark and Bill behind us. "That guy must have had a bad day. I should have been a little kinder. I'd probably growl at late passengers too if I had to do what he does all day. I can't believe those forty-five minutes went that fast. I thought we had plenty of time. I should have watched the time more carefully."

I was dutifully doing penance, and Audra looked annoyed. "Oh, Ruth, you don't need to apologize. You are way too hard on yourself. Give yourself permission to get angry now and then. Everybody else does. Why can't you? It's okay to be late sometimes, too. Now let's enjoy the cruise."

Gradually the bitterness of the day dissolved, and I relaxed. However, I still had a vague feeling that I'd let somebody down. If anyone had asked me, though, I couldn't have told them who it was.

"May I make an observation about you?" Audra's request came as we drove toward an editors' luncheon several weeks later.

Audra and I had been doing some writing for the same publishing house. My most recent deadline had come and gone two weeks before, and my manuscript was still not finished. I'd been apologizing to Audra about my unwise use of time during the last two weeks. "I should have had that manuscript in the mail at least a month ago. The assignment wasn't even that tough. No excuse."

Audra saw past the unfinished manuscript. "Remember the day of the boat ride, that day you apologized for being angry even though I thought you had every right in the world to be angry? Somewhere in your mind you've written, 'I should not get angry.' Today you're apologizing for not being on time. Somewhere on your list of requirements for yourself, you've included, 'I should not be late.' Then when you don't meet your own expectations, you have to apologize.

"Ruth, I don't think your expectations for yourself are realistic. Everyone gets angry sometimes. Everyone is late sometimes. I don't know who you think you have to impress. Maybe it's yourself. But it certainly isn't me. You don't have to be perfect. I wouldn't know what to do with you if you were. Cross some of your unrealistic shoulds off your list. I think sometimes they make you unhappy."

We were driving west, away from the city. Past the prairie grasses that danced on the now-and-then vacant fields. Into semi-suburb driving again. Four-lane traffic. Golden arches. Red, white, and blue gas pumps. Stop. Go. Almost city. But really, I was in the city. Down by the river again. The trend-reversing river. The reflecting river. The revealing river. Images cast upon the waters showed me myself. Not with force, but with gentleness. Not with overbearing callousness, but with delicate care. Evoking not guilt, but gratitude.

I allowed my thoughts to flow aloud. "You're right. Lists of shoulds and oughts for myself and lists of shoulds and oughts for other people. They go together. Long lists. The closer people are to me, the longer the list. Mark. Jori. Nicky. Expectations. Standards. Prescribed behavior. When I disappoint myself, I apologize. When others disappoint me, I criticize. Unrealistic standards, and no one wins." I was focusing aloud in front of Audra. Peeling away the plastic. Reversing the flow.

The next day Audra sent me a little card that said, "I'm glad you're you." Her note was a warm endorsement. Little did I realize how soon I would need its insulation. . . .

Fall came early again. By late October the winds felt arctic. The days were the kind when mothers called their children in early from play, turned the lights on by four-thirty in the afternoon, and plugged up the cracks under the doors with rugs or rolled-up towels. By the beginning of November I'd almost forgotten what it felt like to be warm. I was convinced that my toes and ears would be permanently chilled. But I wasn't prepared physically or psychologically for cold, gray February blasts in November. Nor was I

ready for the soon-to-come personal blasts that would prove much
more devastating than the weather. All in all, November was to be
a cold, cold month.

Audra called one blustery morning just after eight. "This is a
three-minute phone call. Just wanted to check in with you. I know
you have to get the children off to school." Audra's voice sounded
warm over the phone.

"Bill left this morning for the week. Along about Friday, I may
need some cheering up—a phone call, lunch, or some mail. I just
thought I'd warn you in advance. Bill's due in late Saturday night.
With this weather, I'll need all the moral support I can get. Pray
especially that I'll make it through the day with my patience still
intact. I have to work on finances and laundry. You know how
much I enjoy them both. I'm afraid by the end of the day, with no
daddy in sight, that I'll take it out on the boys. I guess you should
pray for them, too. Now, tell me what's on your agenda for today?"

"I'm finishing up an article this morning. Have to go to art
instruction class for the fourth grade at Jori's school at one. Then
this afternoon a neighbor is dropping by. She wants to talk. . . ." I
almost elaborated, but something inside me checked my words.
*Why create a problem if there's not really going to be one? Besides, what would
I say? How would I ask for prayer without sounding like the neighborhood
gossip? Probably, down deep, my pride is at the heart of the matter anyhow.
Neighbors should get along, especially when they're both Christians. They
should be able to work out their differences and difficulties. So their children
fight when they get together. Don't all children? So I have a hard time
understanding her. That's my problem, not Audra's. So I fear a confrontation.
I have to face my fears. Audra can't do it for me. Besides, I've handled
tensions all my life without Audra. Why should today be any different?* So I
gave no hint of where my day could take me. Audra had no way of
knowing.

Christina rang my doorbell at two-thirty. She brought the
November chill in with her. I had the coffeepot ready, and I poured
us both a cup right away. Anything to warm me up inside.

"I've prayed a lot about today," Christina began. My worst
fears were about to be confirmed. I felt the doom descending. "In
fact, two of my prayer partners are praying right now about this

visit. I felt that I had to tell you that I see real problems ahead for you if present trends continue. I've watched a lot of pastors' families. I've seen a lot of pastors' kids who have suffered because their parents are too busy in the Lord's work to be home supervising their own kids. Our children, yours and mine, have their ups and downs when they play together. They argue and fuss. I know that a lot of that is normal—kids will be kids. But I feel that there are some things that you and Mark are too close to, to see in your own children."

I took a very large gulp of my hot coffee. It burned all the way down. In fact, I could feel it stinging my eyes, the pit of my stomach. But still I was cold.

Christina continued. "For example, they are so competitive. It seems to me that something serious is lacking when a child always has to be first, when he has to hurt others to have it his way. I've felt for a long time now that your children are trying to get your attention, but you're too busy to hear or see. That's why they're lashing out at others."

She tapped her fingers nervously on the table top and continued. Her eyes were glued to the wall at a spot just over my head. "As hard as this conversation is for me, if it can save them and you some future pain, then I feel it's worth my coming to you. Sometimes we need other people to help us see things we're too close to, to see for ourselves."

There it was. The river again. Reflecting. Revealing. Showing me images of myself. I believed in it—was convinced that I needed others to create self-portraits for me sometimes. But this time I wanted to run from it. To strike back. To defend myself. To point out all the negative traits I saw in her children, too. To tell her all the times I'd seen them push and shove and butt into the front of the line. To ask her why we'd never shared a cup of coffee during our good times, or how often she'd seen us as an entire family unit, operating together.

Instead, I said what I felt I should say. I thanked her for her concern, asked for her understanding, and vowed to work with her to relieve the tensions between our children.

I sat at the kitchen table for a long time after she'd gone, two empty coffee cups and an empty chair before me. I didn't feel like getting up. The desire to do anything was gone. I'd probably botch whatever I tried to do anyhow. Seemed like I was blowing the most important job in the world. I'd just had sixty minutes of living proof served to me in documented form.

Wonder how many other neighbors are talking to their friends, asking for prayer for me behind my back? Wonder how many other people are praying for this pastor's undisciplined kids? Wonder what Audra really thinks about our family? About my handling of the children?

The whole world suddenly took on a sinister face. It was them versus me. And I was standing alone—alone with my family, the people I loved and cared for more than anything in the world. And I'd just been told I was blowing it with them.

I shivered in the cold. Long after I'd gone to bed that night and even after Mark had wrapped his warm arms around me, I was still shivering. I couldn't get warm, even with the heat turned up and a heavy wool sweater wrapped around me. It's not easy to warm yourself on the inside or to relight the fire while the wind's still blowing.

The sun always shines again, even though the cold remains. The next day was bright and blue on the outside. I turned my desk calendar to Tuesday, November 3. The mechanics of the day were proceeding as usual. Alarm. Shower. Dress. Devotions. Breakfast. Children off to school. But inside I felt disarray, confusion.

Why did she come? What were the feelings behind her visit? What if she is right? What if I am too close to see? What if my blind spot does indeed contain potential tragedy? What is God's opinion and advice? Is it the same as hers? What if others see the same things but are too shy to say so? What if Audra feels this way too, but has never told me?

I turned to Galatians, chapter six, the passage I was teaching this morning in our women's Bible study. I'd prepared it last week without the slightest hint of where I'd be today. "If someone is caught in a sin, you who are spiritual should restore him gently." I leafed through my notes in one final review. This morning they were just pieces of paper with a neat, orderly outline. They were not something I felt. The neat, orderly outline inside me had been sabotaged. But the information was all there for me to teach others.

"Criticism: How to give and take it." I'd done my homework. Waded through lexicons, Bible dictionaries, and concordances looking for the meaning of "restore," "spiritual," "caught." I found that the word "restore" was a medical term for resetting bones—a skill requiring great care and gentleness. I linked the biblical truths with actions to be taken today. Someone would be helped by the morning's discussion. It touched where people hurt.

I gathered my notes, Bible, and overhead transparencies together, engaged my brain in the assignment of the morning, but disengaged my feelings. This morning I did not have the luxury of feeling. The hurt would stay inside, under lock and key—the way it had to be—the way it had always been before.

Driving gave me time to think aloud to God. "Lord, help me stop shivering. There's nothing to be afraid of today. These women are all my friends. I don't want to talk about criticism today, Lord. Not so close to yesterday. But I didn't have time to prepare anything else. They have to be Your words, Lord. I don't have any of my own. What do *I* have to say? Please, Lord, watch over Jori and Nicky."

The tightness returned to my throat. My eyes started to burn. "Dear Lord, I can't cry. Not now. I have to teach a lesson. Bolster me up. I have to talk on criticism. How can I talk on criticism today, Lord? And please help Audra not to call."

Today Audra seemed remote and far away. I didn't want to talk to her. She would know. Right now I could not run the risk of further honesty.

"You look tired today, Ruth. Are you okay?" The Bible study hostess handed me a cup of coffee and a doughnut.

"Oh, I guess I am a little tired. The last couple of days have been kind of rough. But I'm okay. I'll make it. Thanks for asking." I smiled and patted her on the arm. Her sensitivity touched me.

As I drove home later I felt something inside pushing against my restraining walls. My hurt was begging for a doctor but couldn't get to one because it was bound and gagged inside me. All my life I'd had a hard time with people who were always looking for a doctor. *Why don't they fix it themselves? That's what I always do.* And usually it worked, on the exterior anyway. Doctoring my own hurt wasn't nearly so costly, at least in terms of my ego.

I'd do the same with this hurt. Fix it myself. Pray about it. Think about it. Talk about it with Mark. Even prescribe the same medication for my own wound as I often had for others' wounds. Then I'd wait for things to improve. I knew they would. They always did. I would forgive and forget. Time would erase the painful strokes. I called it "toughing it out." Like having a tooth filled without Novocaine. I was strong. I'd make it. I always did.

That night when I went to bed, I was still shivering in the cold.

10

The Journey
Back To Warmth

When the Canada goose wants to escape the cold, he calls his clan together and takes to the air, his long, black neck stretched out in front of him, in a southerly direction. From his Quebec breeding grounds, his five-foot wingspread lofts him as high as eight thousand feet in the air and propels him along at speeds of up to sixty miles per hour, down the Atlantic flyway in search of warmth and food.

Today as I listened to the honking flight information along the V-shaped intercom system high overhead, I wanted to join the migration—to escape the piercing chill and fly away from it all. This year the geese seemed in a bigger hurry than usual. They were flying higher and faster. I felt their urgency. Arctic blasts are hard to live with. I knew.

Then suddenly, as though some internal radar had switched the flight plan, they circled back, into a descent, and cut down through the gray November chill, swooped in just above my head, and glided gracefully onto the park lagoon, still in a V-formation. I could see their white cheek patches and their black, beady eyes. They were not here to stay. I knew they were just "shortstopping"

—a term used in Audubon circles for resting or roosting. Tomorrow they would continue their journey out of the frigid zones and into the temperate. But for tonight at least, they'd have a place of safety and nourishment.

As I rode my bike into the wind, across the two blocks that separated our yard from the park lagoon, I could still hear the gentle stirrings of water behind me. *How gracious of God to provide "shortstopping" for Canada geese—a place to refuel along the route from cold to warmth, a sanctuary where physical needs are met.*

Suddenly I was startled by the obvious contrast—a visual illustration from the skies. *If God so cares for Canada geese, how much more does He care about His children as they pass through the cold, lonely, arctic zones.* Then I saw myself—a lone Canada goose, flying fast and furiously to escape the gray cold. Supporting myself with my own wings—the wings God had given me, strong wings. Trusting my divinely instilled instincts to make the journey to warmth alone. Flying without the formation of others. Refusing the lagoons—the places of safety and nourishment provided for my journey.

Somehow the illustration looked all wrong to me. Canada geese do not fly alone. Never in all the years I'd been watching flying V's in the October to early November skies had I ever seen a Canada goose flying solo. Not because they aren't strong enough. Even a hunter, at home with the ways of the wild, will not venture unarmed near the nesting area where ganders stand guard over mama and her eggs. Ganders can attack sources of danger viciously and brutally.

Nor do Canada geese fly in groups because they aren't smart enough to go it alone. The flight formation of the feathered flock is a social web, complex enough to challenge even the most sophisticated sociologist. Older birds in front. Clans. Families. Groups and sub-groups. Organized with intricate precision, one after another, riding the updraft created by the bird before him, flying in the V-shape so that every bird has a panoramic view.

The journey to warmth should not be made alone. It's easier when you ride the updraft of the one before you—when you are rested and sustained by a friendly lagoon along the way. Canada geese are smart enough to realize they have needs they cannot provide for themselves.

I pushed open the front door at home and wondered why it had taken me so long to catch on. That night I picked up the phone and scheduled morning coffee with Audra.

"So now you know why you haven't heard much from me in the last three weeks. I just couldn't bring myself to tell you about it. Not because I didn't trust you. I guess it's just that I've always kept hurt to myself. It's not easy to change a pattern like that."

Audra had not taken her eyes off me the whole time I was talking, replaying for her my chilling encounter with Christina and the cold, confusing aftermath. The waitress had been to our table three times to offer us refills. We didn't need them; we weren't really there to drink coffee.

Audra waited until she was sure I'd finished before she spoke. "I knew there was something. You've been preoccupied. I felt a door inside you had closed, but I figured you'd open it to me when the time was right. I knew this was one I should not push. You've been hurt, and now you're struggling to sort through it all." Audra was reading my heart. She didn't say anything else for a long time—just looked out the window into a cold, sunny day and thought.

I waited. There was nothing more I could say. I'd risked my reputation as a parent with Audra. Unveiled the tender spots in my self-confidence—my abilities, or lack thereof, at mothering. In a sense, I'd auctioned myself and my children off for inspection—Audra's inspection. I'd asked for her assistance in locating the blind spots. I'd laid bare the hurt and trusted her objectivity to help bring healing.

Finally she spoke. She leaned forward on her elbows, adjusted the two gold chains around her neck, then locked her fingers into each other on the table in front of her. "I have two things I want to say to you, Ruth. One is about the person who came to you, and I'm glad you didn't tell me who it was, and the other is about you. Number one, is this person someone you would go to for advice? And number two, I want to remind you that Bill and I have made you and Mark the guardians of our boys, and someone else has done the same. Evidently there are some of us who think you're doing it right—not perfect, but we believe in your abilities at parenting."

I felt warmth returning to my veins. I needed to hear Audra's perspective. Mark had been too close. Neither of us had thought of asking the question Audra had asked. Nor did we remember that two families had made us guardians of their children—friends who knew us well and had seen the raw ingredients of our lives. I needed Audra's sensitive distance from my hurt to add the logic my emotions had blotted out. I went home feeling warmed and fed by Audra's friendship. Allowing myself to be needy was a new experience for me. . . . Little did I know that soon there would be more times of need.

Baton Rouge, Louisiana, looked sparse and flat from the window of Republic flight 483 from New Orleans. I could see the Mississippi River, crawling like a snake into and out of the rectangular patch of city that squatted on the river's eastern bank. The delta marshlands were already lush, even though winter's frost was still holding the green hostage further north.

I rested my head against the window casing and looked down. My mind was tired, not from the half-hour flight between New Orleans and Baton Rouge, but from the events that had preceded it. Speaking trips were never like a vacation to me, and this one had had an unexpected twist to it—a twist I was still processing in my mind. I knew that most of my tiredness was not physical.

Under most circumstances, New Orleans would have been slow and easy—the casual, comfortable, southern way of doing things. I still had enough southern blood in me to know how it should be. But today as I left the city behind, my insides were churning like the Delta Queen paddlewheeler I'd seen plowing the watery outskirts of the city. Old tensions and pain had been resurrected. I thought I'd laid them to rest forever under the quiet canopy of age and maturity. But here they were, vibrating my insides, as intense and alive as ever.

"What do you think about giving Rick and Lynn a call while you're in New Orleans?" Mark seemed to read my mind as I packed for my trip south. "Don't do it if you think it would be unwise, but it might be a nice way to let them know we haven't forgotten them. Christmas cards don't always do the trick."

Mark understood. He knew where my heart had taken me last time with Rick. But that was yesterday. Rick and Lynn were still friends—the kind you sometimes go out of your way to see, especially when you live a thousand miles apart and you happen to be passing through their town.

"I'll see how my schedule goes. It might be a nice idea, just for old times sake." I gave Mark a quick kiss on the cheek. Our undaunting trust and confidence in each other over the years had been a safe, secure, stable kind of feeling—like having open space within a fence. The boundaries were not usually even an issue. For me, Rick was only a seasonal remembrance—a controlled memory of my past with no significance for the present. Three children. A prospering young church just north and west of New Orleans. Everything was different now.

Almost as an afterthought, I scribbled their address on the envelope of my plane ticket as I hurried out the door to the airport. *Just in case.* My thoughts about them had been casual. Almost too casual. But then, this time I trusted myself. Years have a way of fortifying you. Rick was a chapter I'd finished long ago. Now he and Lynn were just pieces of our early days. People we'd known. Not feelings.

Rick answered the phone when I called from my hotel room at the end of my New Orleans stay. "Ruth Senter. Hey, hey. What a pleasant surprise." I'd heard that same exuberant response before. Years before. Suddenly it seemed that nothing had changed. His voice was still warm and smooth, with a gentle strength about it. Tough and tender. That's how I'd always described him. I heard it today, even over the phone. I tried to picture what a few added years might have done for him.

"So, your plane leaves in two hours and your work is all done." Our conversation had gotten beyond the surface exchange of information—family, what I was doing in New Orleans, his church, Mark's church, my writing.

"Now, how many times do you get to New Orleans? We can't miss an opportunity for lunch once you're here, can we? Lynn and the children aren't here right now, but how about if I give you a ride to the airport. You're on our side of town. I could be at your hotel in fifteen minutes and we'd still have time for a bit of lunch before your flight.''

He was still the same efficient, take-charge Rick. His tone was light and casual, like the Rick of early graduate school days. I momentarily forgot it had been that Rick who'd captured my heart once.

I felt stirrings of uneasiness as I stood before the mirror carefully redoing my make-up. I'd decided to change into my favorite three-piece suit. Why did it suddenly matter? I'd planned on going to the airport the way I was. But that was before the phone call. Now the ride to the airport had a certain significance to it. Similarities. I was feeling them all over again. Why? Don't old feelings die once they are buried. I'd assumed they did. They had been silenced for years. This time things were supposed to be safe. Why, then, did it matter so much all of a sudden?

The minute I saw him walk through the door into the lobby where I was waiting, the years between us collapsed into one brief span. There had been no time. No distance. No separation. He was there, just like he'd been before. The years had subdued him, added a few lines to his forehead and some highlights to his hair. But maturity wore well with Rick. Time had only accentuated his charm. His handshake was warm, his smile just as infectious, his eyes just as blue. I thought they looked more alive than ever. He picked up my suitcase and started toward his car. I noticed that he drove in comfort. The chrome and gray glistened. *A prosperous church, no doubt.*

Rick had always been a good conversationalist. We'd never had trouble talking, and today was no exception. Our conversation was effortless. Natural and comfortable. But I sensed Rick's impatience to get beyond the trivia. I caught his gaze and wondered what he was thinking. What did he remember from the past? What did he think each year when he received our family Christmas photo. I wondered, but I didn't dare ask. Instead I questioned him about his job. I asked about his level of career satisfaction after switching from broadcasting to the pastorate. The minute I asked,

I felt that I'd come one step too close. The wrong question maybe? It was too late to retreat now. I had opened a door.

"Job satisfaction. It's funny that you should use those words." He methodically swirled the ice in his empty water glass. "You know, Ruth, you can't be happy in your job if things aren't happy at home. And things aren't real happy at our house right now. I don't think Lynn ever has accepted the fact that she's a pastor's wife."

No. No. Don't tell me. I don't want to know. Suddenly I felt like I was peeping through a window into which I had no business looking. I didn't belong in this story. There was too much at stake—too many complications of the heart. And yet something in his look pleaded for someone to listen. To understand. I knew I could do both.

Rick leaned forward on his elbows as though looking into the past. His blue eyes were soft. "There was a time when you allowed me to ask some tough questions. Remember? Well, I have another one for you. How do I convince my wife that she's more important to me than my job when she's already made up her mind that I'm married to the church instead of to her? There doesn't seem to be much room for discussing the issue with her. She's visited her mother twice in the last six months." His look changed. His voice dropped—like life was suddenly deflating him. "I don't know what I'll do if my world falls apart, Ruth."

It was a plea—a call for help as clearly and directly as I'd ever heard. Time had created no gap. Rick assumed I'd understand. I sensed his need. I also sensed my power to comfort. I wanted to be his friend. To listen. Encourage. Affirm. Offer insights from my years of marriage to a minister. I wanted to say, Tell me about it. I'll understand. But I didn't. I couldn't. "I guess you've just got to make some sacrifices for her to prove you mean it," was about all I could say. It was time to go.

Rick reached for the bill. There was something sad in his gesture—like he was saying the only thing I could do for him was to let him pay for my lunch. I sensed his aloneness. It drew my heart like a magnet—the heart I had under control. I didn't want to hurry off. He needed a friend—someone to talk to. Someone who

understood. Companionship. But I picked up my suitcase and
headed for Gate F6. Rick was right there beside me, taking my
suitcase from my hand. I saw that he intended to walk with me to
the gate, prolonging the moment.

"Hey, thanks for getting in touch. It's great to see you." There
it was again—that infectious smile. He looked like he was going to
say more, but the final boarding call interrupted him. I took my
suitcase from his hand.

"Thanks for lunch. And, Rick, please make your marriage
work, for everybody's sake." There was no time to say more. I felt
my throat closing up. I'd felt that parting sensation once before—
years before. I walked down the ramp, turned at the door, and
waved. He was still standing there watching me. Alone. A man very
alone.

I could still see his gentle blue eyes and his wide, warm smile
as I closed my eyes and leaned back into my seat on the aircraft. I
needed to leave New Orleans. I needed Baton Rouge. That much I
knew. Baton Rouge was warmth. Security. Understanding. A
stopover. A refuge. A lagoon. A place to rest from my flight into the
wind. Baton Rouge was Audra. She was there with Bill, who was on
a business trip. When she had learned of my trip to New Orleans,
we arranged to meet, since it corresponded perfectly with Bill's
conference in Baton Rouge. It would be short, only twenty-four
hours, but any time together away from the distractions and pressures of home was valuable.

I felt a new sense of need for Audra. When your heart
threatens complications, you need someone to be your head. The
years were teaching me that. I knew Rick was a story that I could
share with Audra. I had no doubts about her understanding. There
would be no sermons, no judgment calls. I trusted her logical gentleness to add insight.

She was there waiting for me behind the glass doors as the
plane rolled to a stop. It suddenly seemed like a long, long time
since I'd seen her. We greeted each other like it had been years
instead of days.

"Tell me all about New Orleans." She slid my suitcase into the
Ford Pinto hatchback from Avis, took the wheel, and navigated the

crosstown expressways like she'd been driving in Baton Rouge all her life.

"Bill will meet us at six o'clock for dinner. He has a tour of the town planned for us tonight—the capitol, the governor's mansion, and the stadium at LSU. I know you're interested in that one." She laughed. "Then tomorrow, until your flight, the day is all ours. There is a wonderful log cabin out in the country where they serve lunch. The vice president of Bill's company told me about it. I think we need to check it out. Mr. Ross said it's the kind of place where you can sit on the front porch and forget there's any other spot on earth."

Mr. Ross was right. The spot he recommended was far from disappointing. The next morning we drove east of town on a narrow, two-lane country road. Sparse lands. Flat lands. Mississippi delta swamp lands. The sky was blue and the ground sandy. The pines stood in patches. Everything else was grass. I thought I smelled salt even though the Gulf of Mexico was some seventy miles due south.

A weather-beaten gray sign leaned against an old creosote fence post. It was almost hidden in the tall grasses, but we caught sight of "The Front Porch" carved in rough, block letters.

"Here's the place." Audra made a sharp turn onto the dirt road that twisted through the pines. Now the sunlight was filtered; the sand was in ruts and very, very dusty. I closed my window to keep out the cloud that followed us.

We started down a little incline and our conversation stopped. We didn't want to interrupt the view. Right in the middle of the pine grove was a natural basin. The lake was blue, its ducks multicolored. Tiny ripples played in the wind and slapped against the tall pines that surrounded it. Just beyond was the cabin—a blend of now and then, old and new. Thick logs, laid one on top of the other, held up a wood-shingled roof and a porch that wrapped itself around the front and sides of the rustic bungalow. We parked the car and moved to the reed rockers that lined the porch. We were the first noon guests.

The birds twittered and the water lapped. Now and then a duck quacked. Everything else was very quiet. A young girl in a

peasant skirt, a blue calico handkerchief tied around her head,
served us fresh orange juice over ice, which we drank from Mason
pint jars.

Audra asked and I talked—about New Orleans, the church at
which I'd spoken and finally about Rick. She never took her eyes
from me. She seemed to sense where my heart might take me.

Now I waited for her to say something. She played with the ice
in her jar and took a long, deep breath—the way she always did
when something big was on her mind. I'd never seen her face look
quite so serious; her dark eyes were misty.

"Ruth, I want you to know that if anything ever happens to
your marriage, it will be your fault. People won't bother to ask
questions. They'll just form opinions. And their opinions will not be
in your favor. You're the one swimming upstream. You're the one
who came to New Orleans to speak. You will pay the consequences
if anything goes wrong."

Her voice wavered with emotion. Her words weren't easy.
"Ruth, you cannot afford to let anything happen to your marriage.
I don't care how many lonely, heartbroken Ricks there are out
there who need your wonderful insights and advice, even if it is an
old friend. Sure you understand about being a pastor's wife. Sure
you wrote a book about it. Sure you could help Rick. But this time
the risks are too high. Stay away from this situation, Ruth. You
have no business helping there."

I could see myself in her eyes. Dear Audra. Brave enough to
hold out the red flag and warn of potential danger. Concerned
enough to cry. Watchful enough to see. Honest enough to speak.
Aware of the damage distractions can do. Willing to sound the
warning. Time would prove Audra right. Rick would stay only a
memory of my past. Casual renewals with him, even in the name of
support and friendship could prove costly. With him, my heart was
too vulnerable. Audra would be my anchor.

There must have been fifty people waiting for the 8:31 flight
from Atlanta when I arrived in Chicago after the final leg of my
journey. I looked into the assortment of faces at the end of the
red-carpeted ramp. Only one face mattered right then. Our eyes
found each other. Then our arms. Welcoming. Wanting arms.

For the next few minutes I was wrapped in Mark's love. I could hear his heart beating as he pressed me close. I was home. Safety. Security. Stability. Man of my covenant. I wanted it this way forever. As Mark and I walked arm in arm through the terminal toward the car, I promised myself that by God's grace it would be. "Forsaking all others" is a very practical promise. This time it took a friend to remind me—a friend who supported me on my journey to warmth and who provided restful stopovers along the way.

11

Storm Clouds Gather

The skies looked ominous. Dark clouds rolled in the west and slashes of light stabbed the earth. The back-yard corkscrew willow and flowering crab bent low against the turbulence, and thunder reverberated between the houses. *Looks like a mean one,* I thought to myself as I went through the house turning on lights and closing windows. There is something unsettling about storms. Uncontrollable. Capricious. Potential cause of uprootedness, displacement. No one knows where the lightning might strike next.

People for centuries have been surviving storms. We'll make it through this one. The thought was somewhat comforting, but I walked through the house feeling very uneasy just the same. I kept my eyes on the western horizon and turned on the radio to follow the weather bulletins. I didn't like the sound of the wind. Its shriek was unfamiliar—a frequency above the status quo.

The status quo. Yes, that was it. Storms threatened the status quo. No wonder I didn't like them. Shifts and rearrangements are hard for me to accept. I like the way things are right now. Comfortable. Enjoyable. Pleasant. Easy. Don't disrupt the flow, snap the power lines, uproot the tree. Keep the clouds in the sky, not on the ground; the rivers in their beds, not in people's basements. Everything in order. Everything in happy permanence.

But once in a while, clouds touch down, rivers run into basements, and trees are yanked from their roots. Once in a while, the earth shifts on its axis and God rearranges. I was soon reminded.

Audra's call came while the storm was still stalking the neighborhood. I jumped at its ring. The wind and Audra's voice were on the same unfamiliar frequency.

"Ruth, you don't need this kind of news in the middle of this storm, but I just got back from the doctor's. My yearly checkup. Ruth, he found a lump in my breast. He says he doesn't like the feel of it. He's referring me to a specialist."

She spoke with an uncharacteristic evenness. She was struggling for control. "I'm tired, Ruth. I don't know how much more I'm up for. It's been a long two months."

Audra had said "help" before during the past eight weeks—not in so many words, but I'd always known what she meant. I'd known how to respond. They'd been minor disruptions then. But cancer did not have a designated slot in my emotions; I had no program for response. Now that the possibility had arisen, I didn't know how to handle the information. File it alongside the facts? I'd collected all the data: last year over 37,000 women died because of breast cancer, and one out of every eleven women develops the dreaded disease.

But Audra was not a statistic. She was my friend—the person who had reached out to me and taken me into her life. Now she was facing the possibility of a massive upheaval. Body cells on the rampage. Audra did not need one more major disruption in her life. Hadn't she already had enough in the last two months?

Lightning ricocheted across telephone lines a couple of streets over. The rain came in sheets and the winds bent it horizontally. Strange that thunder, lightning, wind, and rain all happen at the same time. Symbolic of Audra's life right now.

I thought back. The first hint of transition came in early spring while we picnicked away a Sunday afternoon at the arboretum. The sun shone that day and everything appeared orderly and peaceful. Audra and I watched from our blanket under a sprawling elm while daddies and children tossed frisbees in the air and chased a softball around imaginary bases on an imaginary baseball diamond.

As far as we could see, spring had showered her colors on the trees—pinks, purples, whites, reds, and yellows—arranged in precise harmony so that each one enhanced the beauty of all around it. The conifers, such as the Norway spruce and the eastern hemlock, stayed green forever. The broadleafs changed. I was grateful for the changes spring brought. The brilliant array of color and contrast turned an ordinary picnic into one of nature's spectaculars. Life's changes, however, are not always so welcome.

"Bill and I reached a decision this weekend." Audra volunteered the information. "You know our concern about his job. Well, he's decided to take the five-month training in Atlanta. It seems the wisest course of action at this point. Otherwise, things could be rather precarious." She paused and seemed to be looking into the future. Her jaw was set. Her face determined.

"Five months isn't forever. Added strain. Disorder for a while. But something that has to be. I haven't given myself the luxury of deciding how I feel about it all. At this point it has to be my head, not my heart that rules. I'll make it, but I do know I'll never make it alone." She looked at me when she said it.

"You don't have to." I said without a moment's hesitation. "Tell me what you see me doing for you while Bill's away." The thought of overload never even crossed my mind. I saw the next five months simply as a turn in the road, not as a mountain we had to climb—an unexpected detour, not an obstacle course. It would take us down some new avenues, expose us to some different scenery, but overweight cargo would not damage the carrier.

I had no fears for myself or for Audra. I'd do what I could and leave the rest with Audra and with God. I would stand alongside but not infuse Audra into me. I would feel for her, with her, but not take custody of her. The responsibilities of five months as a single parent ultimately rested in Audra's hands. She and Bill had made the choice together. I trusted their wisdom and released myself from accountability.

But that had been two months ago—before a storm on the

prowl and a lump in her breast. "Lord, lift up Audra." I said it right into the storm as Audra talked. I'd prayed it often during the past two months—at stop signs and red lights. it had been my own little system of support for Audra—a quiet confirmation that what I couldn't do for Audra, I knew God could.

I prayed it when the brake system on her car failed and she had to negotiate a major repair job. "Lord, wrap your arms around Audra for me." I said it right out loud as I walked down the front steps of church one Sunday morning after a brief chat with her. Bill's call the night before had been confusing and unsettling to her. She felt helpless when it came to his needs. Eight hundred miles made intimacy difficult.

"Lord, lift her up." I prayed it when her book negotiations broke down and when Josh had his two front teeth knocked out in a soccer game. "Project your strength into Audra today." I'd felt release even as I said the words. I'd learned the hard way that God didn't intend for me to absorb Audra's load. I did what I could through phone calls, notes of encouragement, and a warm coffeecake from the oven. The rest I left on shoulders far stronger than mine.

At least that's what I'd done in the past. Tonight, however, as the rain pelted everything in sight and Audra struggled with thoughts of breast cancer, I wanted to erect a bulletproof barricade and quickly stuff her inside. Hadn't she already had her share of trouble? *Enough. Stop. One person can only take so much.* I wanted to remind God of man's frailty and to protect my friend from further hurt. But I knew I couldn't. So I said simply, "What is it that you fear the most?"

She had fears. I could tell by her quick response. "Telling Bill. I don't see how I can. He'd hop on a plane and come right home. His course isn't even half over. He can't come home yet. We can't risk having him quit now. Our future is at stake." Only the wind continued through the long pause that followed.

"I'll have to sit this out alone, without him." Her voice blended in with the cries of the storm. Outside a limb snapped on the corkscrew willow. Today it was a weeping willow.

The shifting winds caused the rain to splash in under the

kitchen window and spray against my back. I reached for the window and slammed it shut. You can't control rain. You can only protect yourself from it.

A lump in my breast. How would I feel? My hand pressed against my ribs and worked its way up. Two aunts dead of breast cancer. I felt for the symptoms.

"You're scared right now, Audra, aren't you? Feeling alone, overwhelmed, and overloaded. What can I do for you?"

"Just let me struggle. Don't condemn me when I tell you I feel picked on. Why this? On top of everything else. I can't afford it right now—mentally, or physically. Doesn't God know that? Doesn't He keep timing in mind when He sends storms?"

I realized she was not asking questions, so I waited. "I don't know what I'll do about telling Bill. Maybe I should just wait and see what the tests reveal. A mammogram is set for Monday. Yes, there is something you can do for me besides what you're already done tonight. I need a picnic in the park tomorrow—providing the storm passes—and a place for the boys on Monday morning. My appointment is at nine o'clock. I need to go now, Ruth, and spend some time with the boys. You've done what you can for the present. Just pray me to sleep. I'll check in with you in the morning about the picnic."

Her voice faded out. The storm moved in on the telephone lines. I felt it all around me now. It sparked at the transmitter in the back yard and snapped off the lights. In the gray I rummaged through a drawer and found a candle. It was a feeble light against the dark, but the children and I ate our tuna salad sandwiches by it and played a game in its shadow. Storms are not something you plan for in advance. Neither are power losses. But when they come, you make the best of the light you have.

I did that tonight as I got ready for bed in the dark. There's no fighting the storm. No worrying it away. I'd do what I did the other 364 nights of the year. Brush my teeth. Wash my face. Go to bed. The storm would pass and morning would come. At least that was one thing I could count on.

"Lord, there's nothing we can do but wait for the tests." I listened to the churning winds. "Tonight I can do nothing for her but go to sleep. Wrap your arms around her. Remind her of what she already knows about You and teach her the things she doesn't. Restore us through sleep, both of us, so we'll have strength for tomorrow—whatever it brings. And, Lord, my friend doesn't really belong to me. I can't hang on to her or keep her safe. That's Your department."

I made the rounds and kissed the sleeping children, the way I did every other night; then felt my way to the doors and double-checked the locks, the way I did every night when Mark was gone. And then I slept—a peaceful, quiet, refreshing sleep. In the morning we gathered up the broken tree limbs and uprighted the patio furniture that the wind had played havoc with. One storm had ended.

The next few days we waited for test results like a defendant waiting for the verdict. We were waiting while we picnicked at the park with the children. They streaked up and down, across and over, under and above. Slides. Swings. Seesaws. Corkscrew shoots. I wished aloud I could harness even one-third of that energetic flow for myself.

Audra sat on her yellow and orange lounge chair, her knees drawn up, her arms wrapped around them. She was wearing yellow but she looked subdued. Serious. Melancholy. Remnants from the picnic were neatly packed away in the baskets, and the red and white checked tablecloth was wiped clean. Our evening chores were done. She leaned back and stared off into the distance—above the playground clatter and commotion. The merry-go-round squeaked under the jumble of piled-on bodies—flying legs, arms, and feet; the children squealed with laughter and delight.

Audra was in another world. "Ever thought how much of life isn't what you planned? You have these rosy dreams of what the future will be, and when you get there it's gray. So much of my life has been unexpected. Life keeps throwing me curves. It's those things I can't control that I struggle to accept sometimes, Ruth. Sometimes I feel like I'm hanging in suspension, waiting to see where God will strike next. But God's not that kind of God is He?"

The children were building a pyramid now—a wiggly, shaky,

construction of human forms. They'd collected a few extra play-mates, enough bodies for four abreast, then three, then two. Kingpin number one was cautiously working his way toward the top. The collapse had been planned. One bottom anchor man sim-ply decided to roll over. The downfall was uproarious. Painless. A pile of cheers and shouts. The caved-in pyramid picked itself up and started to build all over again. Human pyramids were built to fall. The triumph came in rebuilding. Audra appeared not to have noticed. Other things were on her mind.

"Have you ever wondered how God chooses who gets the pain in life? Sometimes the distribution seems disproportionate to me. You trust God with your life and you suffer. You obey and you're squeezed through the press. You dedicate your children to Him, and your reward is a handicapped child. You submit and you end up with a lump in your breast."

Her thoughts seemed to stop in midair—almost like she felt she'd said too much. I kept my eyes on her and leaned forward to encourage her to continue. The words were hard for her, I knew, but they expressed the honest struggles of her heart. She reached out her arm in my direction.

"Oh, Ruth. Thank you for not quoting Romans 8:28 to me. I know that verse and every other one in the Bible about God's good and perfect and acceptable will. I believe them with my head, but right now I don't feel they're true. God's will doesn't feel right and good and it's certainly not acceptable to me—yet. It feels unfair, unjust, and terribly unreasonable."

She paused and looked directly at me. This time she saw me. "But you know. You've been here. Different hurts. Different ques-tions maybe. But the same pain. I guess that's why I don't feel condemnation from you. The Lord knows I don't need guilt right now, too."

She shivered and pulled her jacket up around her shoulders. The evening had almost disappeared; all that was left of the sun were streaks of pink out over the lagoon. The children were feeding the ducks from the bag of bread crumbs we'd brought along. Audra stood and moved toward the table. She sat down on the bench next to my chair.

"Thanks, Ruth. I'll pull out of this. I sure am glad God will still be around tomorrow when I'm feeling better."

It was time to go. I folded my lawn chair and propped it at the end of the picnic table. "I guess any relationship we're committed to has its risks, Audra, including ours with God." There didn't seem to be a need to say anything more, so I didn't. Audra nodded her silent agreement, and we started for home. In the west the sun had gone down and we were left to walk in gray.

The gray didn't go away. It only lightened for a while. Variegated gray. Gray skies. Gray clouds—above and below. Gray when the fog touched down at night. Gray in the Russian olive tree planted in the neighbor's back yard. Not Audra's gray. My own gray. Non-color mixed with a sense of impending mutation. The unsettling storm had settled within.

There were splotches of color here and there, now and then. The doctor's report was encouraging—at least for the moment. Only a muscular cyst that needed watching. No immediate danger. We celebrated with lunch on the patio. My red geraniums were in full bloom. The windmill that kept the crows out of my garden was a blur of spinning yellow, and the tomatoes hung on the vine, lush and red. Audra laughed a hearty chuckle when I read her a "Life in These United States" story from *Reader's Digest,* and we both smiled with motherly pleasure at the childish negotiations taking place over a third-base dispute in the whiffleball game. It was a rosy moment.

There was color in the middle of the next week, too. Deep purple, yellow, and white fused together in a delicate silver vase. "A book celebration," Audra called it, at the Little Traveler, a collection of shops and restaurants housed in a seventeenth-century Victorian mansion along the Fox River. It was probably my favorite eating place in all the western suburbs. Audra knew that. That's why she chose the spot to host her celebration of the new book contract I'd signed two days earlier.

"It's not every person who gets to commemorate her friend's new book. I'm not about to miss the opportunity. I'm proud of you and your books. Why shouldn't we celebrate?" She was handing me the bouquets even though negotiations for her own book had broken down, even though the lump in her breast hadn't gone away, and even though her husband hadn't returned from Atlanta. We were celebrating. Color in the midst of gray. Success was sweetened by the affirmation of a friend.

"You're a natural writer, Ruth. I believe you have lots more books in you. So here's to your many future books." She lifted her iced tea glass in a toast. My eyes misted and my throat choked up. True celebration of *my* success. Genuine. Sincere. No fear that she'd come in second. No boycott of another's victory. No threat that her own gifts and talents would be diminished by another's success. No penalty for achievement. No infringing on another's moment of glory. The moment was mine. Audra had created it for me and reserved its significance for my triumph. It brought back memories of other days and other times when success was not so sweet. I looked across the table into sterling friendship.

After we finished our cheesecake dessert, Audra handed me a little package wrapped in blue. The Hadley pottery bowl inside was to hold this day in memory. Little did I realize how soon I would have to depend on memories and how soon I would be left to walk in the gray again—at least for a while.

12

Transplanted

The tiny tentacles clung fiercely together, resisting outside interference. I dug my fingers gently into the clods of dirt that protected the root system and pried the delicate subterranean spines apart.

"Your marigolds are ready to transplant," my neighbor-horticulturist observed across the back-yard fence one day. I was surprised. They looked full and healthy to me—a solid mass of deep green, topped off with brilliant yellow. Why disturb them?

"They're at the stage where they'll grow better if you separate the root systems and spread them out a bit." I looked skeptical. "You'll see," she said wisely. "Sometimes with plants you have to destroy to give space to grow." Her yard and garden bore evidence that there was a tiller of the soil who knew what she was talking about, so I submitted to her wisdom and dug up my beautiful row of marigolds.

Uprooting a system I'd so carefully cultivated made me feel like I was working in reverse. The solid fortress of strong green and yellow was gone, and in its place were sparse stalks scattered along the dirt. Isolated. Vulnerable. Susceptible to nature's force. "Space to grow," my neighbor had said. "That's what the pulling apart will give your plants." It was a prediction of things to come.

But I wasn't ready for it so soon—just three years after it began. The human drama of pulling up roots. Ripping apart the system. Closing out the gentle years. Today I felt the ache deep inside me as I moved through Audra's half-empty house. I removed the watercolor bird prints from her family room wall. The soaring birds were Canada geese, wild and majestic. They reminded me of Audra, my support system. Flying the updraft so I could face the winds head-on. A safe lagoon from November's chill. A haven from New Orleans' heat.

I carefully wrapped the prints in a triple thickness of brown packing paper and settled them gently into the box for their thousand-mile ride to North Carolina. I felt like I was wrapping my support system in a triple thickness of brown packing paper. It would be stored away in a corrugated box for another place, another time—a time when someone else would need it. I didn't remember that God's support comes, not in flesh and blood, but in Spirit. Right now I was struggling with finality—physical separation. Spiritual bonding was something Audra and I would learn in our future apartness.

Today that finality had settled in—like the gray fog that sits on the lagoon on misty days. Two weeks and Audra would be gone. The house had sold in ten days. Bill's new job would begin November 1. Today was October 15. I looked ahead. November —non-growth. Non-color. Unending. Gray, cold November—the month that always seemed to settle inside me. This year it already had, and there was no spring in sight. Audra's pending departure blotted out the seasons, at least temporarily.

Audra gone. Taken by the whim of corporate management. My harbor of safety, moved to a new location. My celebrations and bouquets, Godiva chocolate and white sailboats, Chicago River and apple orchards, ripped from their roots, never to be again.

I'd learned to trust, to risk, to unfold petals long since closed by winter's cold. With Audra, I'd cautiously lifted my face toward the sunlight and drank deeply of its rays—gentle and warm. Springtime. God's gift of a friend. Now, like some giant hand playing yo-yo, that gift was being snatched up, away, leaving only the shell of memories, devoid of the substance, reminiscent of pain.

I picked up the Austrian crystal Christmas tree—the one that had sparkled the colors of the rainbow on the night of wassail and holly, hemlock and fruit cake. Today it sat on a basement shelf along with other Christmas decorations, waiting to be packed. I lifted it from its tissue-paper nest and turned it in the light. The rainbow colors were still there, but today I associated them with pain, not a party.

I buried the colors beneath the tissue, a white gift box, more paper, and then settled it into a packer's box—brown and sturdy. It would be protected from jolts and jostles, careless handling, and sudden stops.

I'd do the same with my emotions next time. Bury them deep in a nest of white tissue paper. That way they wouldn't get broken by the sudden starts and stops of life. Emotions are delicate—as fragile as Austrian crystal. You leave them out in the open and they're bound to be broken, one way or another. Don't grow too close and the separation won't hurt as much. Don't sink your roots too deep and the extraction will be less painful. I'd return to protecting myself in the future, the way I'd done before.

But today the ripping apart was excruciating. Everywhere I looked in Audra's house alterations were taking place—alterations that accentuated the happy times gone by. The inevitability of change. Hard reality when it was taking your friend from you. But inevitabilities are part of nature's flow. God's decrees. You compensate by bottling up the hurt. At least, that's what I did for a while. I left Audra's house by the back door, trying to avoid walking past the "Sold" sign in the front yard. I didn't talk about moving day.

But the countdown ended. The day arrived. We met at a favorite little pastry shop. I stirred my coffee and tapped my spoon on the edge of my cup. I tried hard to pretend that this was just another coffee time with Audra. We'd have our pecan roll, check in with each other about the week's progress, plans for the future, and then we'd go home until the next time—a phone call, a quick drop-in, a celebration on the patio, passing in the hallway at church, candlelight dinner for four, a Saturday night double-date at the movies. There'd be more. Lots more after this. But I knew it wasn't true. While we were drinking our coffee, the moving van was waiting in Audra's driveway, loaded and ready to go. Bill and the boys were turning in the house keys to the realtor. Things wouldn't be the same ever again. Why pretend?

What do I say? I didn't trust my voice to say much. I spoke softly and took deep breaths in between. Audra played with the two gold chains that dangled gracefully over her burgundy sweater. She looked amazingly orderly for being in the midst of upheaval.

"This isn't the end, Ruth. It's just the beginning of something new. We thrive on challenges. I think that's one reason we found each other in the beginning. We'll adjust, we'll find new ways of caring for each other." She paused. We were both struggling for control. "But that doesn't change the fact that I'm going to miss you deeply. There's going to be a big vacancy."

Neither of us trusted ourselves to say anything else, so we paid our bill at the cashier's booth and walked toward our cars in the parking lot out back. I'd bought a book for Audra—about friendship, wrapped it in blue and brown plaid paper, and signed it, "In the midst of change, some things remain forever. Lovingly, Ruth." I handed it to her now and trusted my written words to do the communicating.

"One last token." From the back seat she took her green schefflera plant, the one that had been in her living room from the very beginning. I'd watched it grow. "Symbolic of our friendship." She handed it to me and gave me a hug. We clung to each other for a moment and then she was gone. I watched her blue station wagon drive out of the parking lot. It was loaded for the trip south.

There was nothing to do but get in the car and drive home. The traffic moved by me in rapid, almost panicked succession. All in a hurry to go somewhere. Horns tooted. Trains crossed the tracks in front of me. The postman drove the shoulder, delivering mail in his little red, white, and blue truck. Gas attendants pumped gasoline into empty tanks, and men in three-piece business suits hustled in and out of offices. Life was going on as usual. It seemed a mockery. Life wasn't that casual. That carefree. That uncomplicated.

Inside, people hurt. They suffer loss. They feel emptiness. They struggle to keep their balance when the earth shifts under their feet. They cry when the hurt gets too great—right in the middle of dinner, with their family seated around them, while they feed themselves lasagne, tossed salad, and garlic bread, they break down and cry.

Mark got up and put his strong arms around me. Supportive and tender. "I know it hurts, honey. Go ahead and cry. North Carolina seems a long way away, doesn't it?"

I put my head on his shoulder. Neither of us spoke, but my thoughts were racing. *Why? Why did God give me a taste of what true friendship is all about, then snatch it away from me? It took me so long to learn to trust, so many conversations to learn to tell the truth about myself, so many years to realize I needed a friend. . . ."*

My tears came unashamedly—a gush of grief over what had been and was no longer. *She knew what to do and what not to do for me. She understood even before I said anything.*

Suddenly I felt tired. I had no resistance to tears any more, no desire to rebuild ever again. Mark sat down in his big wing chair and pulled me down on his lap. We sat there until my grief worked its way out, at least for that time. Then he brought me a cup of hot tea, and I went to bed. Somewhere in the night a blue Pontiac wagon and a moving van headed south, away from me.

"It's okay, Lord. It's okay," I cried into my darkened bedroom. "Sometimes marigolds grow best when they're uprooted. Sometimes they need the space. Lord, I want to grow. I want the same for Audra. But please, Lord, don't ask me to risk again, ever—at least for a long, long time. It's just too painful for me when it ends." Then I went to sleep and dreamed that a storm had uprooted our back-yard corkscrew willow. . . .

November was empty. I looked for Audra through the gray. Someone else sat in her place at church. Someone else's car was parked in the driveway of her house. Someone else drove a blue Pontiac wagon and wore blues and browns and burgundy sweaters with two gold chains around her neck. I looked, but it was always someone else—someone who didn't even look or act or sound like Audra.

Then one frosty, January morning the phone rang. I thought of Audra. She sometimes called around this time.

"Ruthie, how'd you like to do a big favor for your brother?" Only my family called me "Ruthie."

"Anything for you, Denny." Calls from my family were always like sunshine in the gray, especially when they came on a colorless January morning.

"One of our church families just moved within five miles of you. I talked to them last night on the phone. Their moving van arrived yesterday. They are special people. Four children, including a two-year-old with cerebral palsy. Vicki needs a friend, Ruthie. I told her you'd be calling. Here's her number."

My hand shook as I scribbled down the number. *Not yet, Lord. I'm not ready yet. The dirt is still fresh from the last uprooting—piled up around the hole left by the tree that was so recently torn away. Besides, that place is for Audra. No one else can ever fill it.*

After Denny's call I sat at the kitchen table, sipped on peppermint tea, and stared out across the gray day for a long, long time. At noon I picked up the phone and dialed the number. Any other way, I knew now, was far too lonely. Audra's place would never be taken. Our friendship would continue, would be strengthened by space and time. But other vacancies now needed filling. Not replacements. Only additions.

God had created me to risk loving and being loved. That's how He had done it. "For God so loved . . . that He gave. . . ." High risk—for me. I had yet to love that much, yet to hurt that much, yet to lose that much for someone else.

Vicki answered the phone.

And thus began another cycle. A new growing season. Another season of friendship.